Arise

SCRIPTURE REFLECTIONS

Mary and Carman Lando

LitPrime Solutions
21250 Hawthorne Blvd
Suite 500, Torrance, CA 90503
www.litprime.com
Phone: 1-800-981-9893

Published by LitPrime Solutions   03/16/2023

ISBN: 979-8-88703-157-6(sc)
ISBN: 979-8-88703-159-0(e)

Library of Congress Control Number: 2023902034

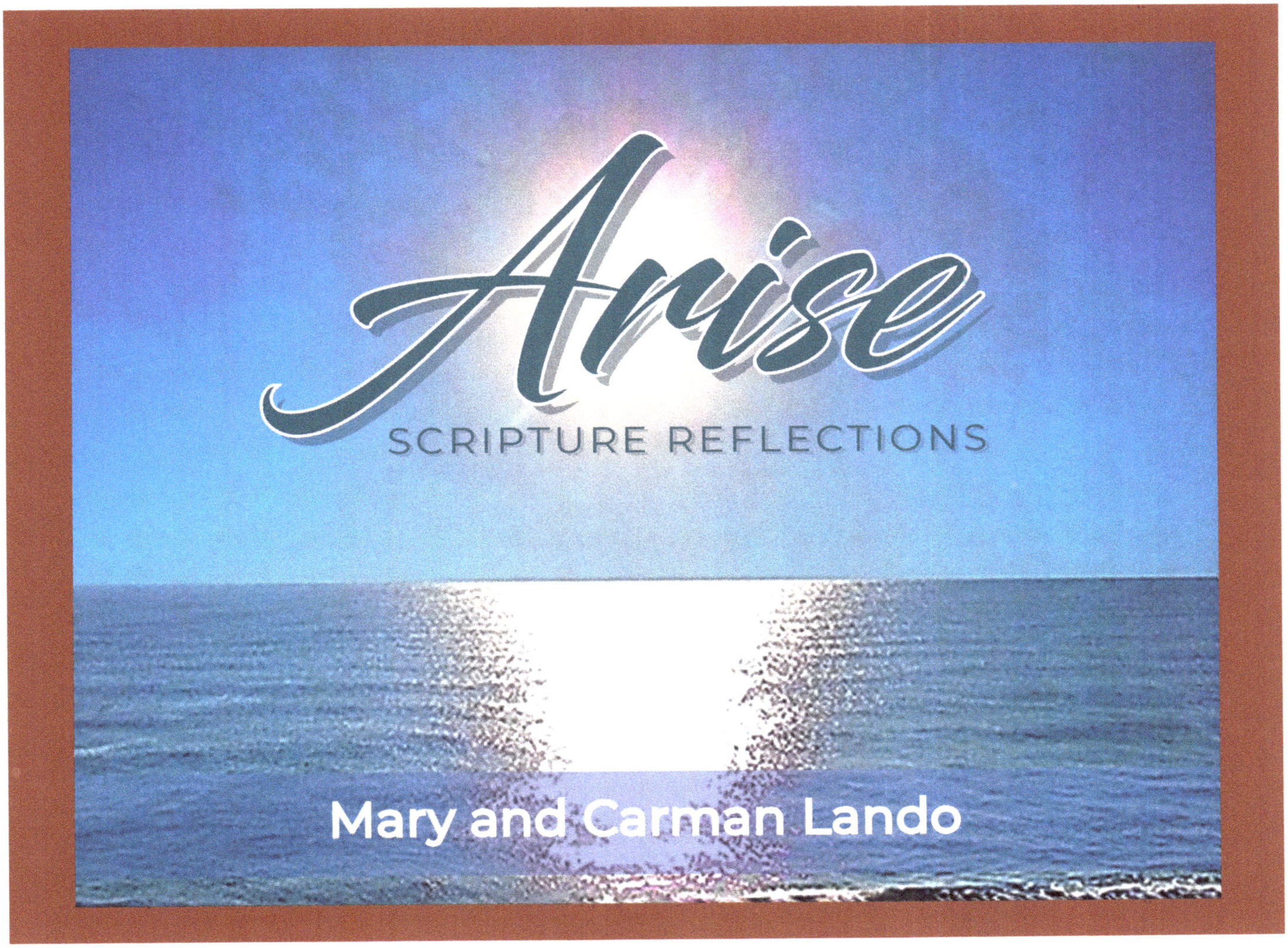

Arise
SCRIPTURE REFLECTIONS

Mary and Carman Lando

Spirit-Fire ministry began in 1990 in order to share God's Love and message of hope through music and Scripture.

My wife Mary and I have served in many parishes in the Archdiocese of New York as well as in other States.

We have shared our music at: Masses, youth rallies, coffee houses, concerts, reflective evenings and charismatic conferences.

Through reconciliation, parish community, and embracing the Sacraments, I was able to receive new wine in these old wineskins.

"God is Good," all the time!

I released the book, "Arise, Scripture Reflections" to further share our faith with the wider Body of Christ. We have been blessed, and continually receiving strength that God has given us through His Son Jesus Christ, with the love of the Holy Spirit, to evangelize His Church through our marriage.

We received the Sacrament of Marriage in 1985, February 17. We have been serving together since 1983 and encountered many anointed Priests who have enabled us to embrace a living relationship with Our Lord and Savior, Jesus. To see beyond the bread that we eat, and to strengthen ourselves in the Body and Blood of Jesus Christ present in the Eucharist.

Ministry in Jesus Christ is a calling of great responsibility. The Sacraments, especially Eucharist Adoration, has been the driving force behind our anointing. Thanks be to God for the out-pouring love of our Priests and communities in which we have served.

If you would like us to share our ministry and or to order our book, "Arise, Scripture Reflections," in your parish please call: (845) 235-5541, (914) 474-8072 or e-mail us at: mlando1208@aol.com

May God Bless your day, Mary and Carman Lando.

In the Name of the Father, and of the Son, and of the Holy Spirit.
Our Father, Who art in heaven,
hallowed be Thy Name.
Thy Kingdom come. Thy Will be done,
on earth as it is in Heaven.
Give us this day our daily bread.
And forgive us our trespasses,
as we forgive those
who trespass against us.
And lead us not into temptation,
but deliver us from evil.

Hail Mary, full of Grace, the Lord is with thee.
Blessed art thou among women, and blessed is the fruit
of thy womb, Jesus. Holy Mary, Mother of God, pray for us
sinners now, and at the hour of death. Amen!

In the beginning was the Word,
and the Word was with God,
and the Word was God.
He was in the beginning with God.
All things came to be through him,
and without him nothing came to be.
What came to be through him was life,
and this life was the light of the human race;
the light shines in the darkness,
and the darkness has not overcome it.

John 1:1-5

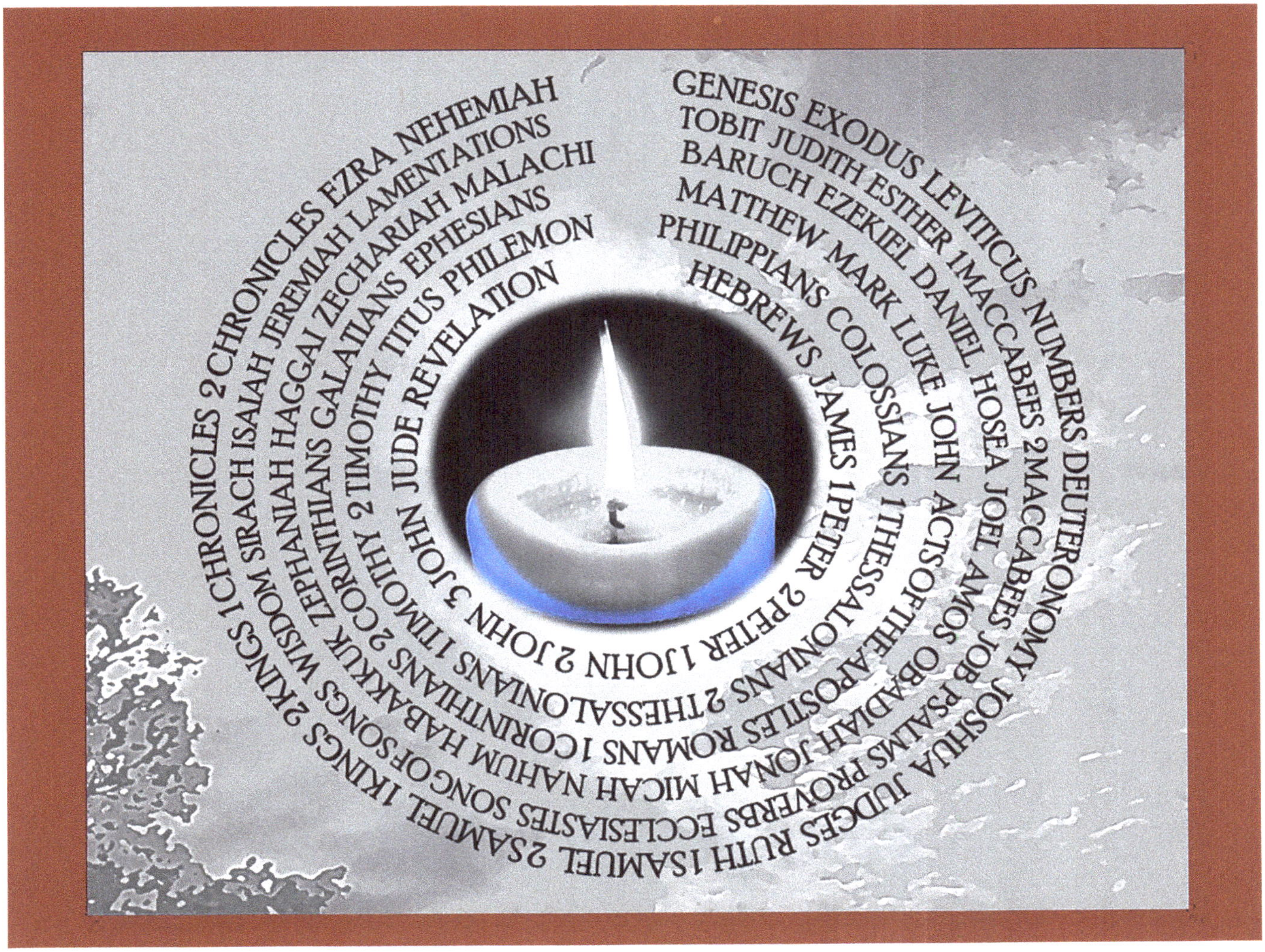
GENESIS EXODUS LEVITICUS NUMBERS DEUTERONOMY JOSHUA JUDGES RUTH 1SAMUEL 2SAMUEL 1KINGS 2KINGS 1CHRONICLES 2CHRONICLES EZRA NEHEMIAH
TOBIT JUDITH ESTHER 1MACCABEES 2MACCABEES JOB PSALMS PROVERBS ECCLESIASTES SONGOFSONGS WISDOM SIRACH ISAIAH JEREMIAH LAMENTATIONS
BARUCH EZEKIEL DANIEL HOSEA JOEL AMOS OBADIAH JONAH MICAH NAHUM HABAKKUK ZEPHANIAH HAGGAI ZECHARIAH MALACHI
MATTHEW MARK LUKE JOHN ACTSOFTHEAPOSTLES ROMANS 1CORINTHIANS 2CORINTHIANS GALATIANS EPHESIANS
PHILIPPIANS COLOSSIANS 1THESSALONIANS 2THESSALONIANS 1TIMOTHY 2TIMOTHY TITUS PHILEMON
HEBREWS JAMES 1PETER 2PETER 1JOHN 2JOHN 3JOHN JUDE REVELATION

Wisdom Understanding Counsel Fortitude
Knowledge Piety Fear of the Lord

Gifts of the Holy Spirit

I love you, Lord, my strength,
Lord, my rock, my fortress, my deliverer,
My God, my rock of refuge,
my shield, my saving horn, my stronghold!
Praised be the Lord, I exclaim!
I have been delivered from my enemies.

Psalms 18:2-4

Fear not, I am with you;
be not dismayed; I am your God.
I will strengthen you, and help you,
and uphold you with my right hand of justice.

Abba

Isaiah 41:10

And so it begins,

Victory over death!

We believe in the Holy Spirit the Lord
the giver of life who proceeds from the
Father and the Son,

who with the Father and the Son
is worship and glorified,
who has spoken through the prophets.

Eucharistic Adoration

Resurrection Victory

Whoever belongs to God,
Hears the Word of God!

Love

Truth

Forgiveness

John 8: 47

I give you a new commandment:
love one another as I have loved you.
So you also should love one another.
This is how all will know
that you are my disciples,
if you have love for one another.

John 13:34-35

You, Lord, give light to my lamp;
my God brightens the darkness about me.

Psalm 18: 29

Tear drops of love from Heaven

And he will send out his angels
with a trumpet blast,
and they will gather his elect
from the four winds,
from one end of the heavens
to the other.

Matthew 24:31

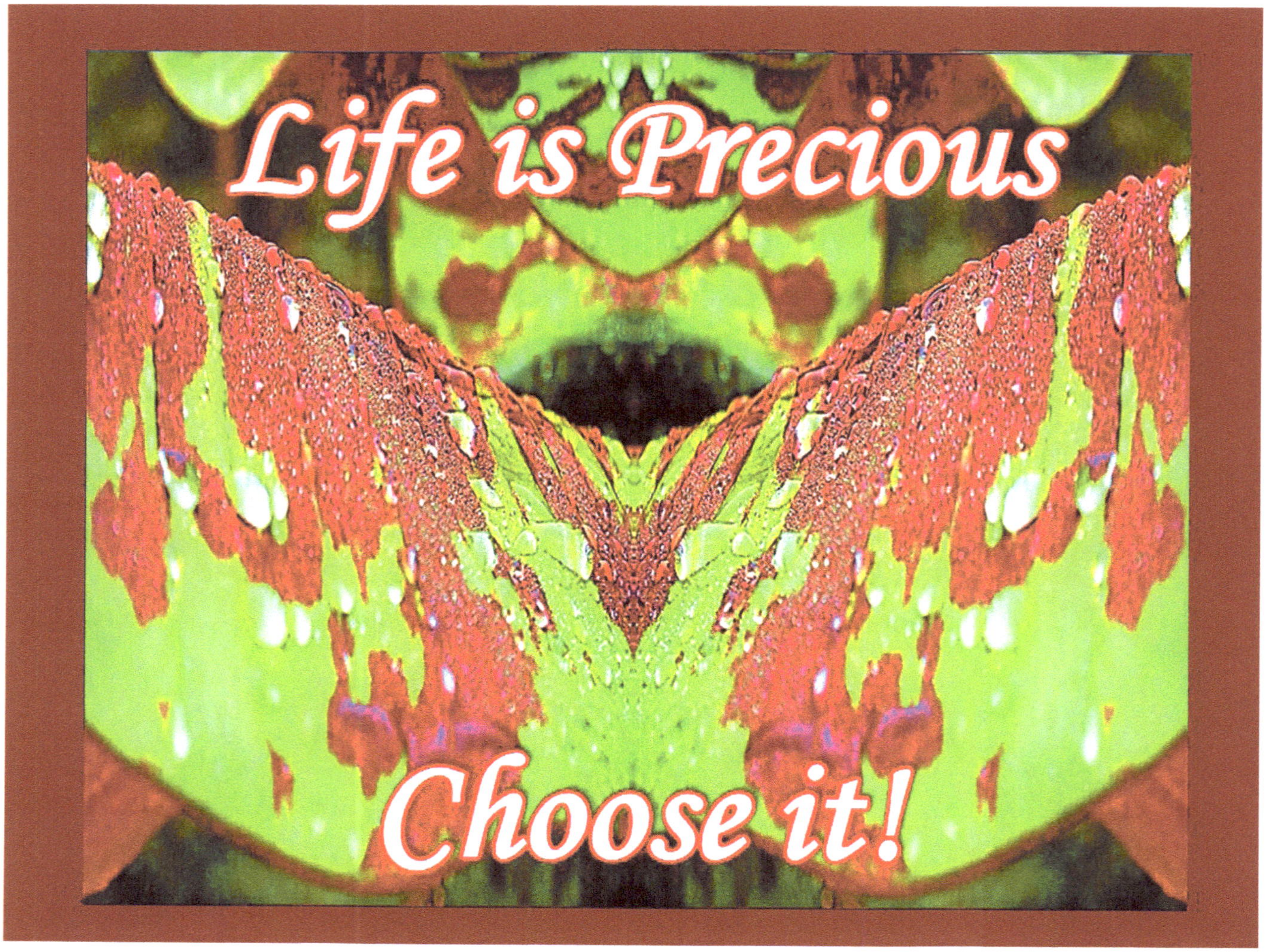
Life is Precious
Choose it!

Jesus spoke to them again, saying,
"I am the light of the world.

Whoever follows me will not walk in darkness,
but will have the light of life."
John 8:12

I am baptizing you with water, for repentance, but the one who is coming after me is mightier than I. I am not worthy to carry his sandals. He will baptize you with the Holy Spirit and Fire. Matthew 3:11

Mercy is Falling

Blessed are the merciful,
for they will be shown mercy.
Matthew 5:7

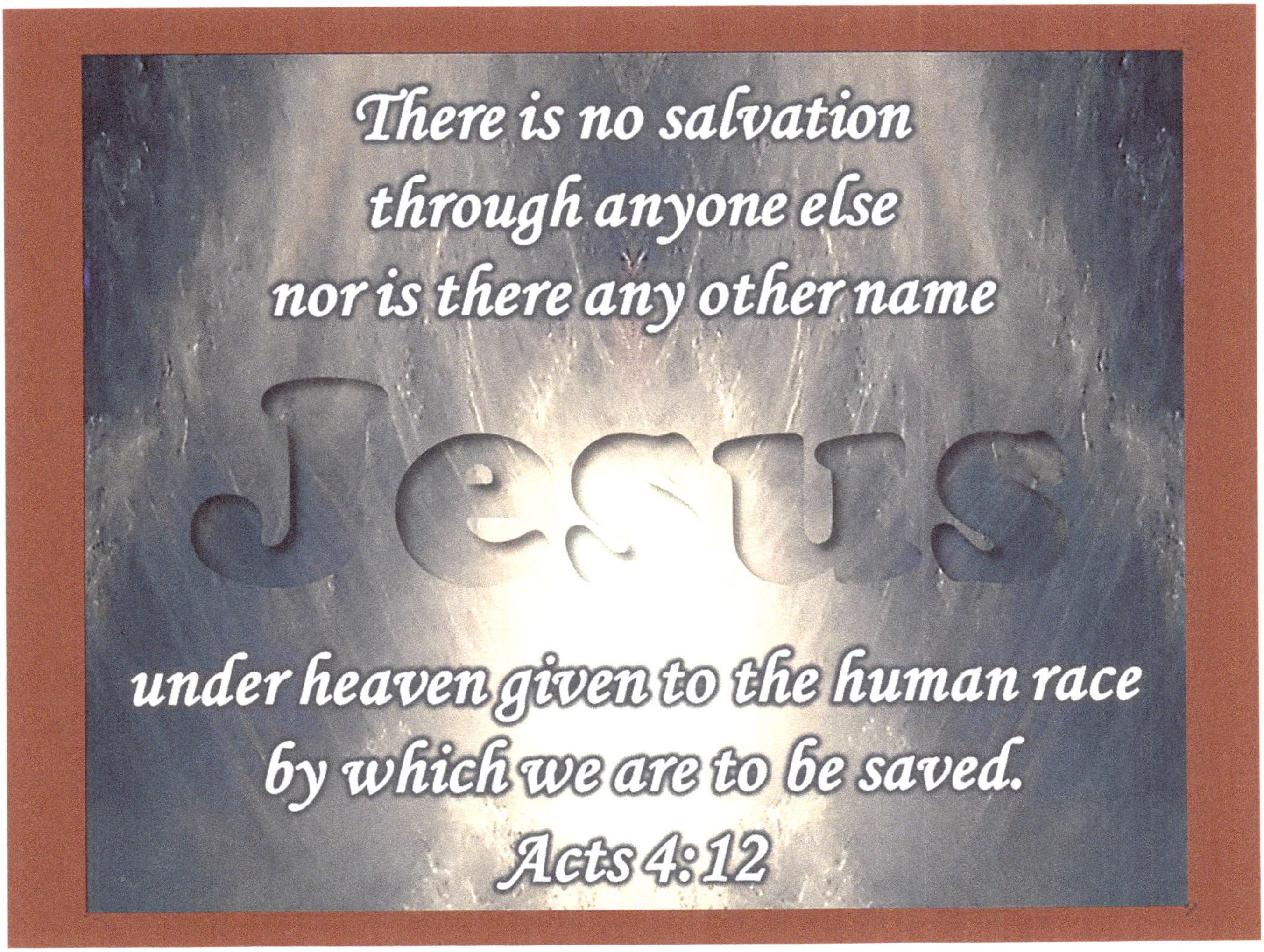

There is no salvation
through anyone else
nor is there any other name

Jesus

under heaven given to the human race
by which we are to be saved.

Acts 4:12

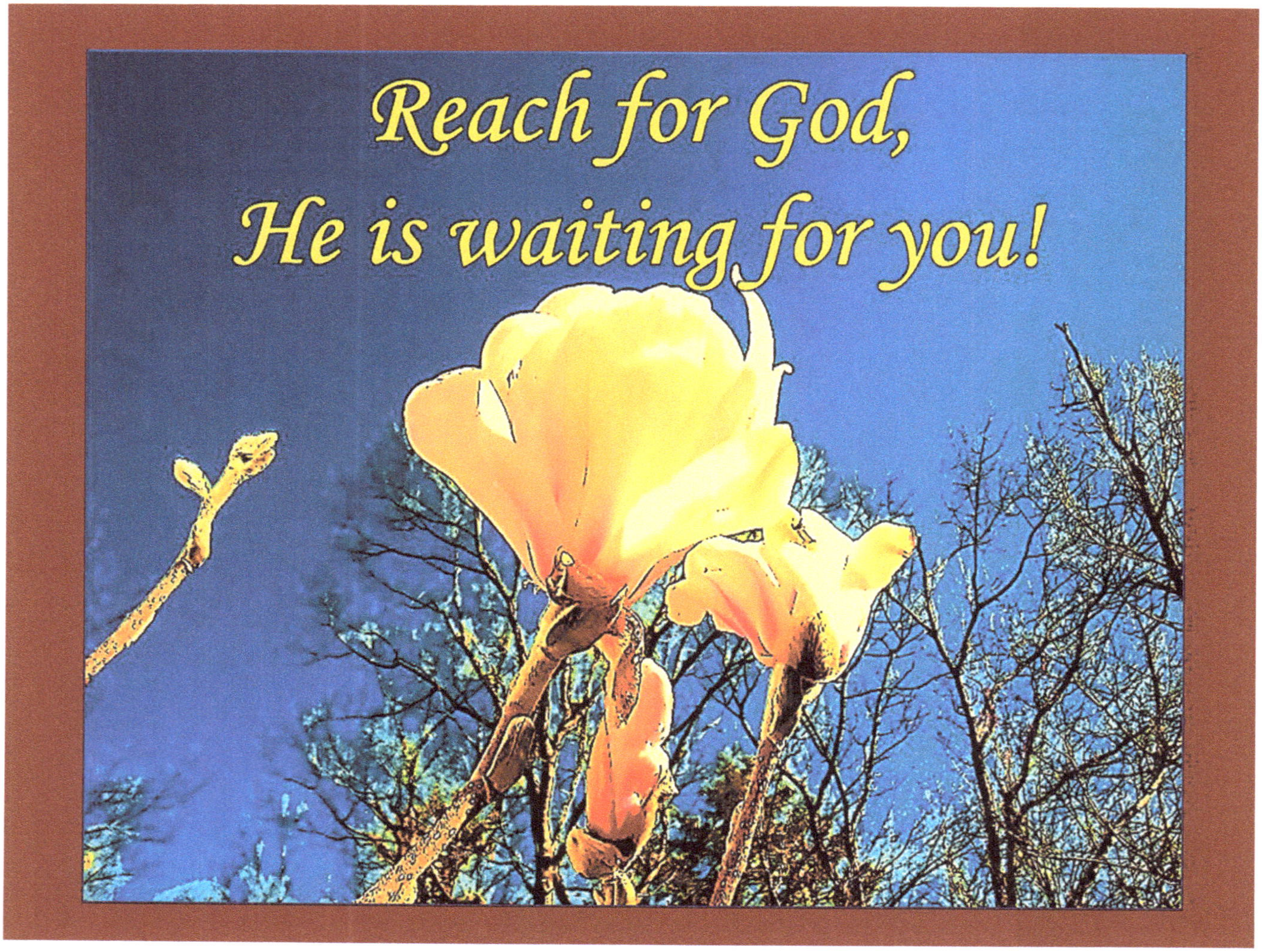
Reach for God,
He is waiting for you!

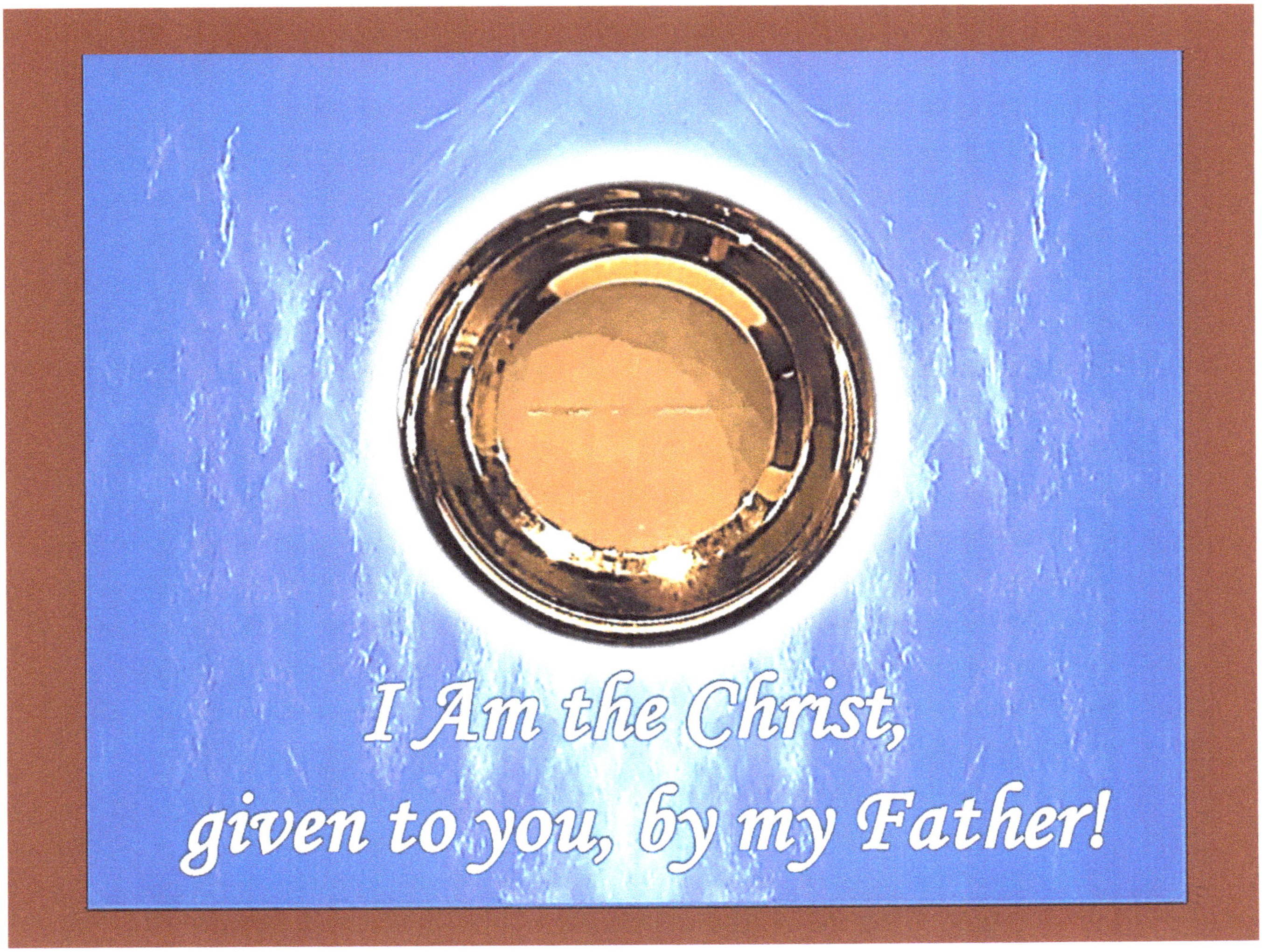

I Am the Christ,
given to you, by my Father!

Everyone shall be saved who calls on the Name of the Lord.
Acts of the Apostles 2:21

Jesus

Know that I love you.
Know that I am within you.
Know that I go before you.

Go, therefore, and make disciples of all nations,
baptizing them in the name of the
Father, and of the Son, and of the holy Spirit,
teaching them to observe all that I have commanded
you. And behold, I am with you always,
until the end of the age."
Matthew 28:19-20

The Lord is my light and my salvation;
whom do I fear?
The Lord is my life's refuge;
of whom am I afraid?

Redeemer

One thing I ask of the Lord; this I seek:
to dwell in the Lord's house
all the days of my life.
Psalm 27:1,4

Love is patient, love is kind.
It is not jealous, is not pompous,
it is not inflated, it is not rude,
it does not seek its own interests,
it is not quick-tempered, it does not brood over
injury, it does not rejoice over wrongdoing
but rejoices with the truth.
It bears all things, believes all things,
hopes all things, endures all things.
Love never fails.

1 Corinthians 13:4-8

"I Am"

The centurion said in reply,
"Lord, I am not worthy
to have you enter
under my roof;
only say the word
and my servant will be healed.

Matthew 8:8

As you go, make this proclamation:
'The kingdom of heaven is at hand.'
Cure the sick, raise the dead, cleanse lepers,
drive out demons.
Without cost you have received;
without cost you are to give.

Matthew 10: 7-9

Awareness of the End of Time

And do this because you know the time;
it is the hour now for you to awake from sleep.
For our salvation is nearer now than when we first
believed; the night is advanced, the day
is at hand. Let us then throw off the works
of darkness [and] put on the armor of light.
Romans 13:11-12

As he passed by the Sea of Galilee, he saw Simon and his
brother Andrew casting their nets into the sea;
they were fishermen. Jesus said to them,
"Come after me, and I will make you fishers of men."
Then they abandoned their nets and followed him.
He walked along a little farther and saw James,
the son of Zebedee, and his brother John.
They too were in a boat mending their nets.

Then he called them.

Mark 1:16-20

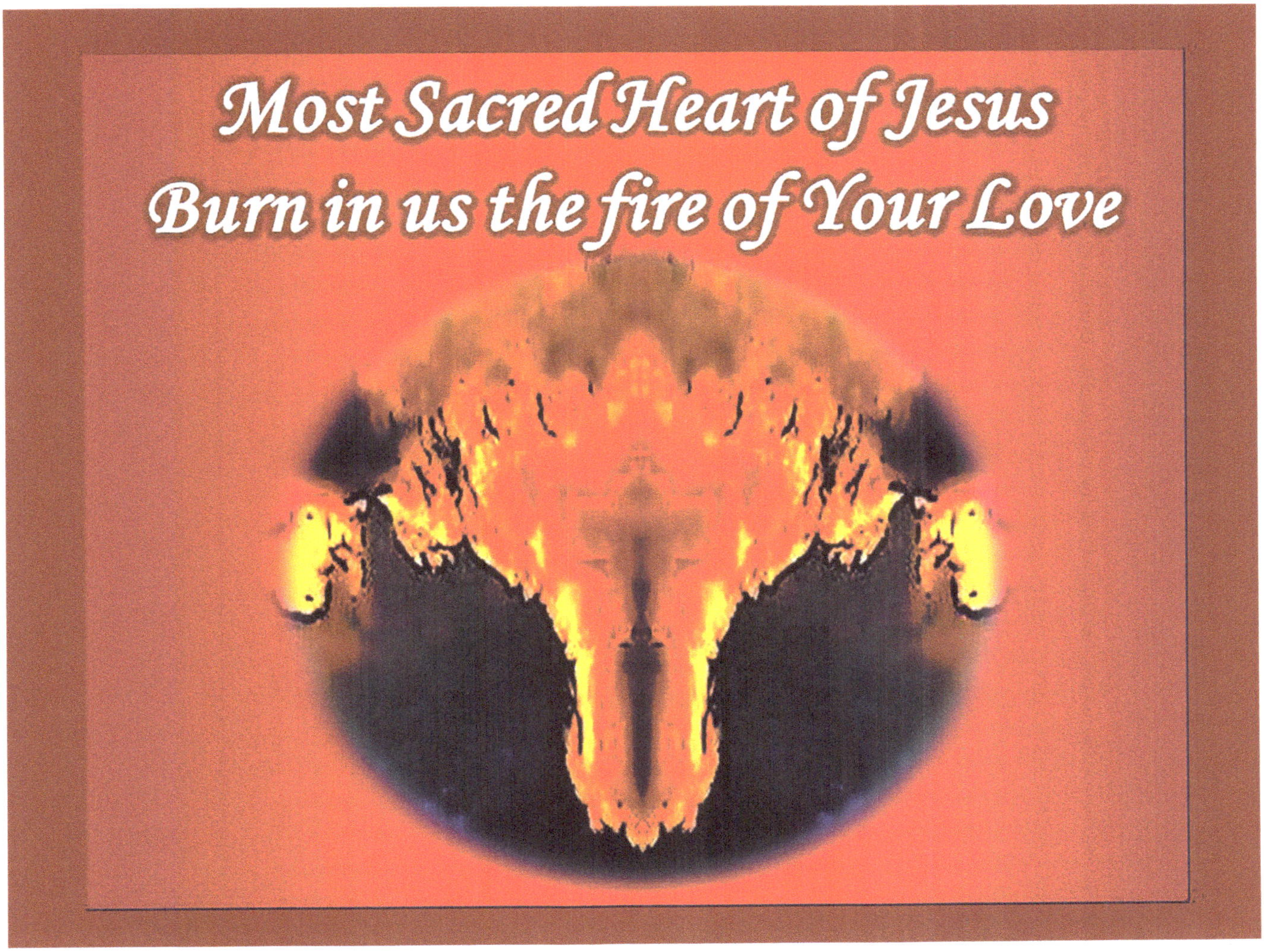
Most Sacred Heart of Jesus
Burn in us the fire of Your Love

When Jesus saw his mother and the disciple there whom he loved, he said to his mother, "Woman, behold, your son."

Even then, I knew your name

Then he said to the disciple, "Behold, your mother." And from that hour the disciple took her into his home.   John 19:26-27

Dying You destroyed our death!

Rising You restored our Life!

All stops lead to Christ!

I Believe in God,
the Father Almighty,

Creator of Heaven and Earth!

When you call me,
when you go to pray
to me,
I will listen to you.
When you look for me,
you will find me.
Yes, when you seek
me with all your heart,
you will find me
with you, says the Lord.
Jeremiah 29: 12-14

In the Silence
of my heart,
I seek You,
My Lord!

Blessed be the God and Father
of our Lord Jesus Christ,
who has blessed us in Christ
with every spiritual blessing
in the heavens, as he chose us in him,
before the foundation of the world,
to be holy and without
blemish before him.

Ephesians 1:3-4

You formed my inmost being; you knit me in my mother's womb. I praise you, so wonderfully you made me; wonderful are your works!

My very self you knew, my bones were not hidden from you, when I was being made in secret, fashioned as in the depths of the earth.
Psalm 139:13-15

Behold, he is coming amid the clouds, and every eye will see him, even those who pierced him. All the peoples of the earth will lament him. Yes. Amen.

"I am the Alpha and the Omega," says the Lord God, "the one who is and who was and who is to come, the almighty."
Revelation 1:7-8

He is the stone rejected by you,   the builders, which has become the cornerstone. There is no salvation through anyone else, nor is there any other name under heaven given to the human race by which we are to be saved.   Acts 4:11-12

Jesus Jesus Jesus Jesus Jesus

Jesus Jesus Jesus Jesus

Jesus Jesus Jesus Jesus Jesus

Jesus Jesus Jesus Jesus

There is no fear in love;
Perfect love drives out all fear.

1 John 4:18

It is not that I have already taken hold of it or have already attained perfect maturity, but I continue my pursuit in hope that I may possess it, since I have indeed been taken Possession of by Christ [Jesus].

Brothers, I for my part do not consider myself to have taken possession. Just one thing: forgetting what lies behind but straining forward to what lies ahead, I continue my pursuit toward the goal, the prize of God's upward calling, in Christ Jesus.

Philippians 3:12-14

Genesis - Revelation

We have God's Word for it's Truth!

Alpha - Omega

Jesus is Lord of All!

If then you were raised with Christ,
seek what is above,
where Christ is seated
at the right hand of God.
Think of what is above,
not of what is on earth.

Colossians 3:1-2

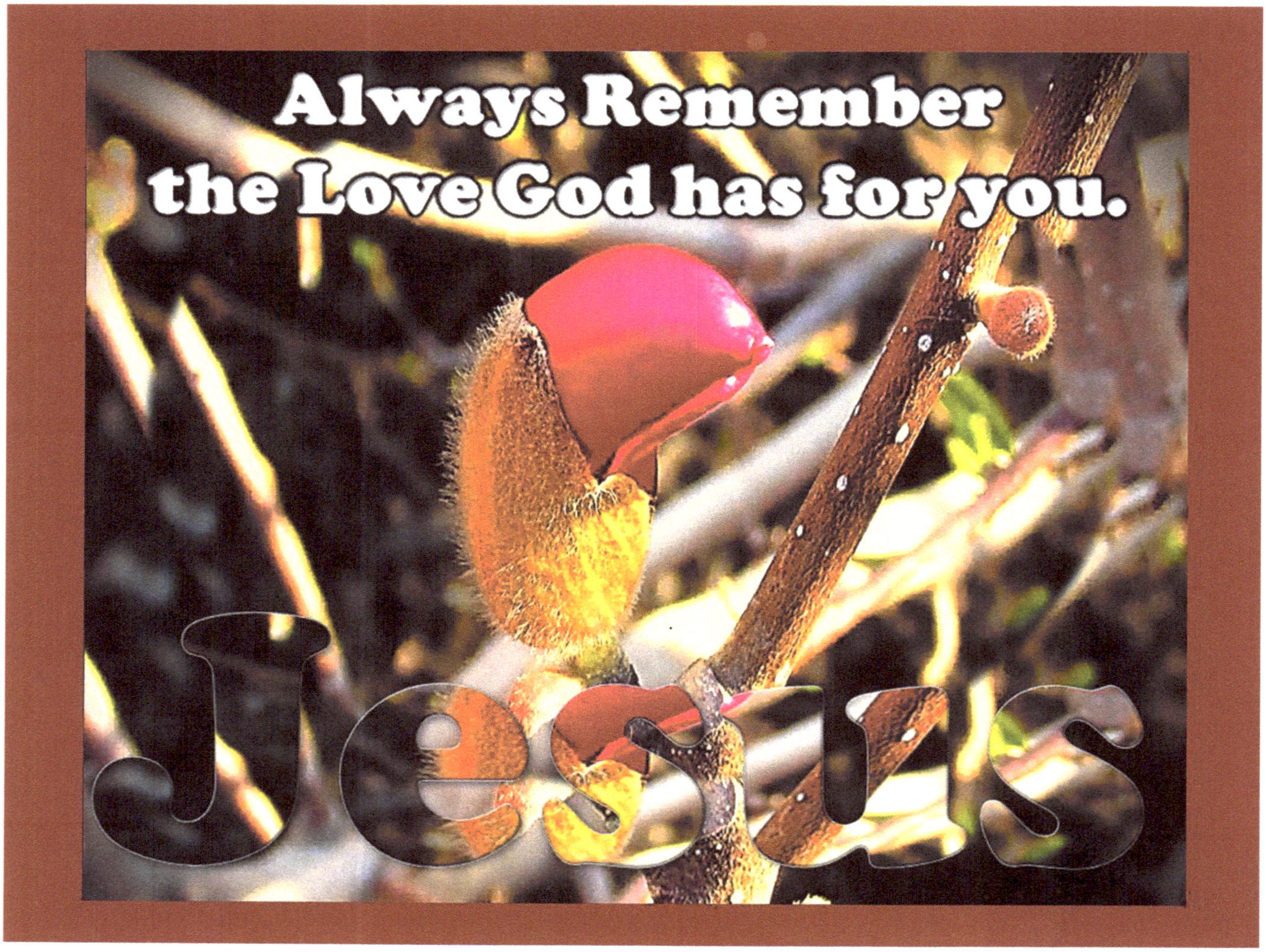
Always Remember
the Love God has for you.
Jesus

I am here for all to see!

What I say to you, I say to all *"Watch!"*
Mark 13:37
Then from the cloud came a voice that said,
"This is my chosen Son; *Listen* to Him!"
Luke 9:35
As they were proceeding on their journey someone
said, "I will *Follow* you wherever You go!"
Luke 9:57

Watch!   Listen!   Follow!

Through the ministry of the Church may God give you pardon and peace, and I absolve you from your sins in the Name of the Father, and of the Son and of the Holy Spirit.

Lay your burdens down!

**Choosing God
and living by that choice,**

**will make all the difference
in your life!**

When you spread out your hands,
I close my eyes to you;
Though you pray the more, I will not listen.
Your hands are full of blood!
Wash yourselves clean!
Put away your misdeeds from before my eyes;
cease doing evil; learn to do good.
Make justice your aim: redress the wronged,
hear the orphan's plea, defend the widow.

Isaiah 1: 15-17

When you call me, when you go to pray to me,
I will listen to you. When you look for me,
you will find me.

Yes, when you seek me with all your heart,
you will find me with you, says the Lord.
Jeremiah 29: 12-14

For God did not give us a spirit of cowardice but rather of power and love and self-control. So do not be ashamed of your testimony to our Lord, nor of me, a prisoner for his sake; but bear your share of hardship for the gospel with the strength that comes from God.

2 Timothy 1:6-7

Covenant

Relationship

The Advocate, the Holy Spirit that the Father will send in my name, he will teach you everything and remind you of all that I told you. Peace I leave with you; my peace I give to you. Not as the world gives do I give it to you.

John 14:26-27

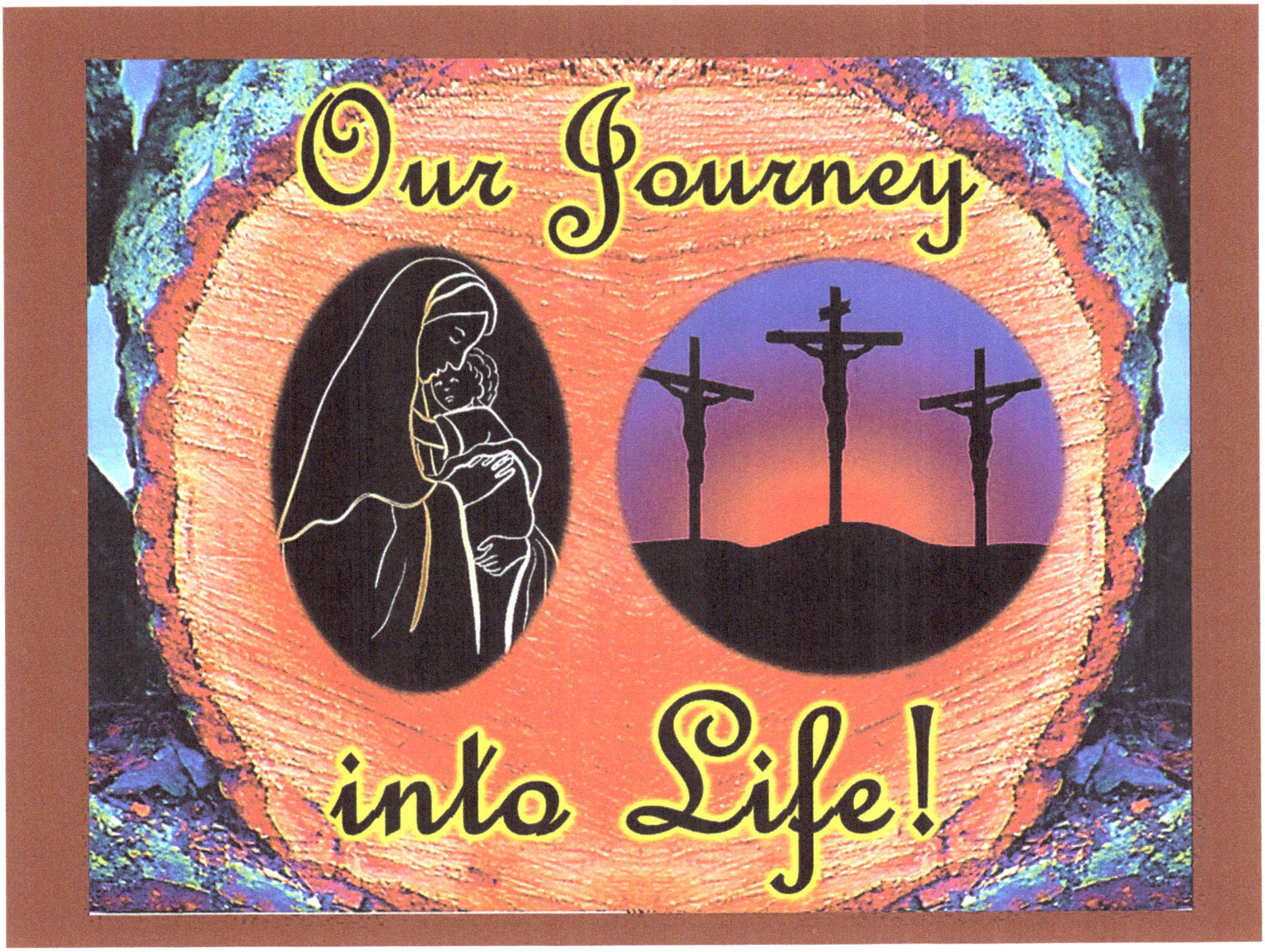

Our Journey

into Life!

But you, beloved,
build yourselves up in your most
holy faith;
pray in the Holy Spirit.
Keep yourselves in the love of God
and wait for the mercy
of our Lord Jesus Christ
that leads to eternal life.

Jude 1:20-21

The Lord is in his holy temple;
the Lord's throne is in heaven.
God's eyes keep careful watch;
they test all peoples.
The Lord tests the good and the bad,
hates those who love violence,
and rains upon the wicked fiery coals
and brimstone, a scorching wind their
allotted cup. The Lord is just and loves
just deeds; the upright shall see his face.

Psalm 11: 4-7

I am the vine, you are the branches. Whoever remains in me and I in him will bear much fruit, because without me you can do nothing. Anyone who does not remain in me will be thrown out like a branch and wither; people will gather them and throw them into a fire and they will be burned. If you remain in me and my words remain in you, ask for whatever you want and it will be done for you. By this is my Father glorified, that you bear much fruit and become my disciples. As the Father loves me, so I also love you. Remain in my love. If you keep my commandments, you will remain in my love, just as I have kept my Father's commandments and remain in his love.
John 15:5-10

"I call heaven and earth today to witness
against you:
I have set before you life and death,
the blessing and the curse.
Choose life, then, that you and your descendants
may live, by loving the Lord,
your God, heeding his voice, and holding fast to him.
For that will mean life for you,
a long life for you to live on the land
which the Lord swore he would give to your fathers
Abraham, Isaac and Jacob."

Deuteronomy 30: 19-20

We are all different!
We are all God's Children!

"No journey to freedom happens
Without the grace of God,

and the power of His Holy Spirit
working in and through you."

The fruit of the Spirit is love,
joy, peace, patience, kindness,
generosity, faithfulness,
gentleness, self-control.
Now those who belong to Christ [Jesus]
have crucified their flesh
with its passions and desires.
If we live in the Spirit,
let us also follow the Spirit.

Galatians 5:22-25

Do you not know that your body
is a temple of the Holy Spirit
within you,
whom you have from God,
and that you are not your own?
For you have been purchased at a price.
Therefore glorify God in your body.

1 Corinthians 6:19-20

Hail Mary, full of grace, The Lord is with Thee. Blessed art thou among women, and blessed is the fruit of thy womb Jesus. Holy Mary, Mother of God, Pray for us sinners, now, and at the hour of our death, Amen.

By His Death and Resurrection
He has set us Free!

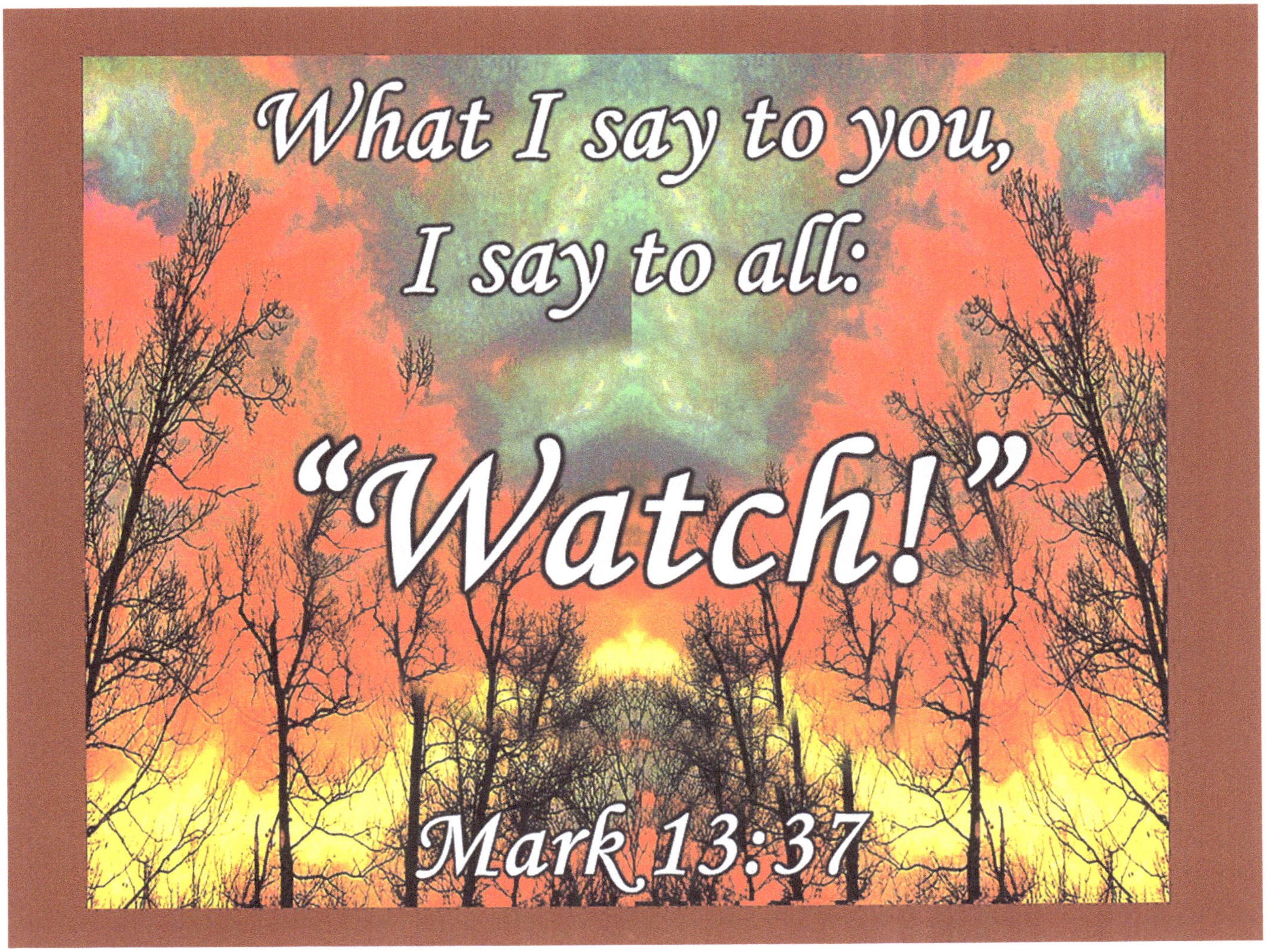

What I say to you,
I say to all:

"Watch!"

Mark 13:37

Seven "I Am" Sayings in John's Gospel

1. Bread - "I am the bread of life; he who comes to Me shall not hunger."
      John 6:35

2. Light - "I am the light of the world; he who follows Me shall not walk
      in the darkness, but shall have the light of life." John 8:12

3. Gate - "I am the gate; if anyone enters through Me, he shall be saved,
      and shall go in and out, and find pasture." John 10:9

4. Good Shepherd - "I am the good shepherd; the good shepherd
      lays down His life for His sheep." John 10:11

5. Resurrection and Life - "I am the resurrection and the life;
      he who believes in Me shall live even if he dies." John 11:25

6. Way, Truth, Life - "I am the way, and the truth, and the life;
      no one comes to the Father, but through Me." John 14:6

7. True vine - "I am the true vine, and My Father is the vinedresser."
      John 15:1

Praise Worship

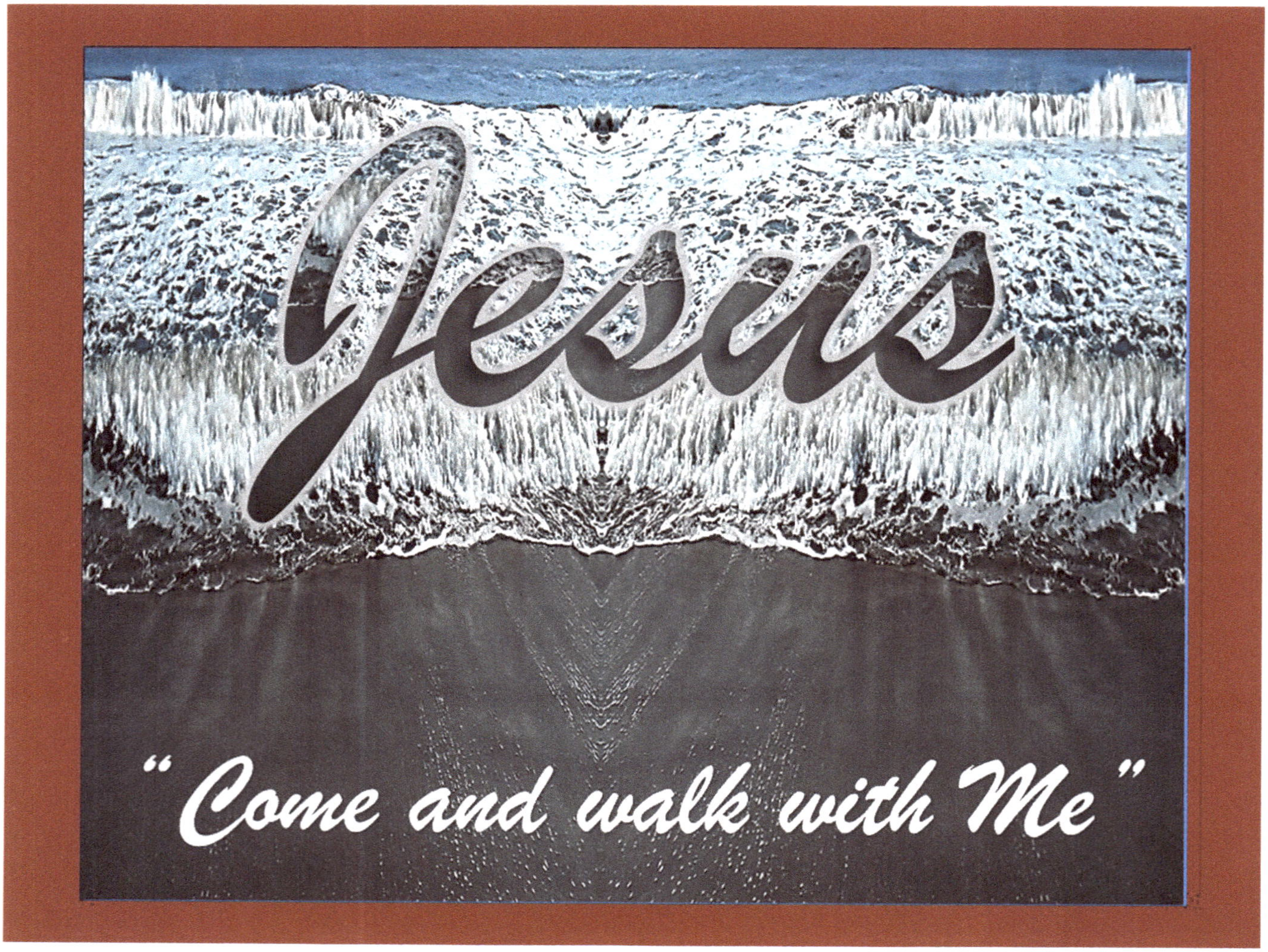
Jesus
"Come and walk with Me"

Put on then, as God's chosen ones, holy and beloved, heartfelt compassion, kindness, humility, gentleness, and patience, bearing with one another and forgiving one another, if one has a grievance against another; as the Lord has forgiven you, so must you also do. And over all these put on love, that is, the bond of perfection.

Colossians 3:12-14

Abba

Jesus said, "Abba, Father,
all things are possible to you.
Take this cup away from me,
but not what I will
but what you will."
Mark 14:36

I will place my law within them,
And write it upon their hearts;

I will be their God,
and they shall be my people.
Jeremiah 31:33

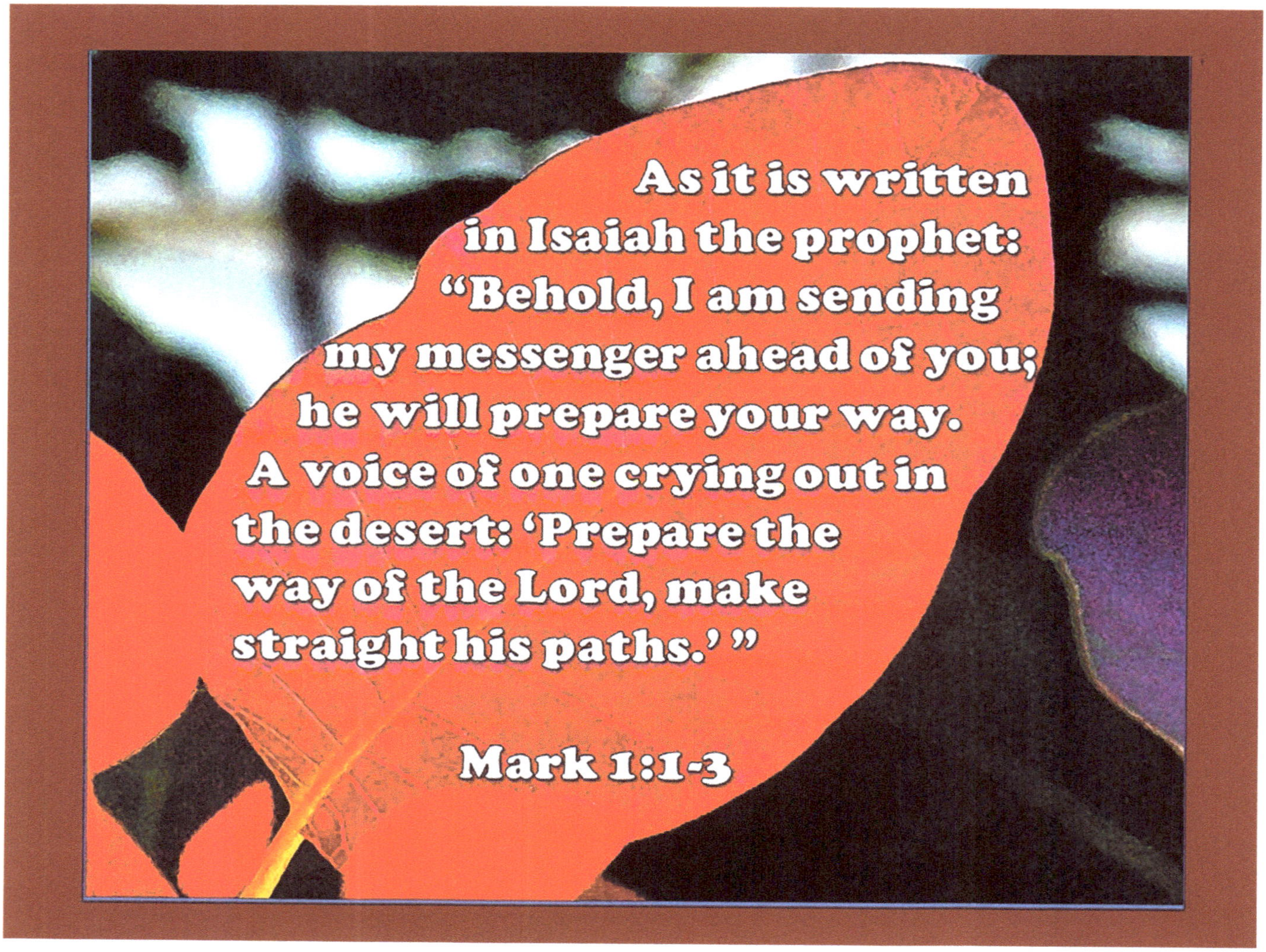

As it is written in Isaiah the prophet: "Behold, I am sending my messenger ahead of you; he will prepare your way. A voice of one crying out in the desert: 'Prepare the way of the Lord, make straight his paths.' "

Mark 1:1-3

Lord, make me an instrument of your peace.
Where there is hatred, let me sow love;
where there is injury, pardon;
where there is doubt, faith; where there is despair, hope;
where there is darkness, light;
and where there is sadness, joy.
O Divine Master, grant that I may not so much seek
to be consoled as to console;
to be understood as to understand; to be loved as to love.
For it is in giving that we receive;
it is in pardoning that we are pardoned;
and it is in dying that we are born to eternal life.
Amen

Where will your decisions take you to?

THE CROSS?

(OR)

THE WORLD?

"Let your "YES" mean "YES," and your "NO" mean "NO."

There is no fear in love;
perfect love drives out all fear.

1 John 4:18

Then he took a cup, gave thanks, and gave it to them, saying, "Drink from it, all of you, for this

is my blood of the covenant, which will be shed on behalf of many or the forgiveness of sins.
Matthew 26: 27-28

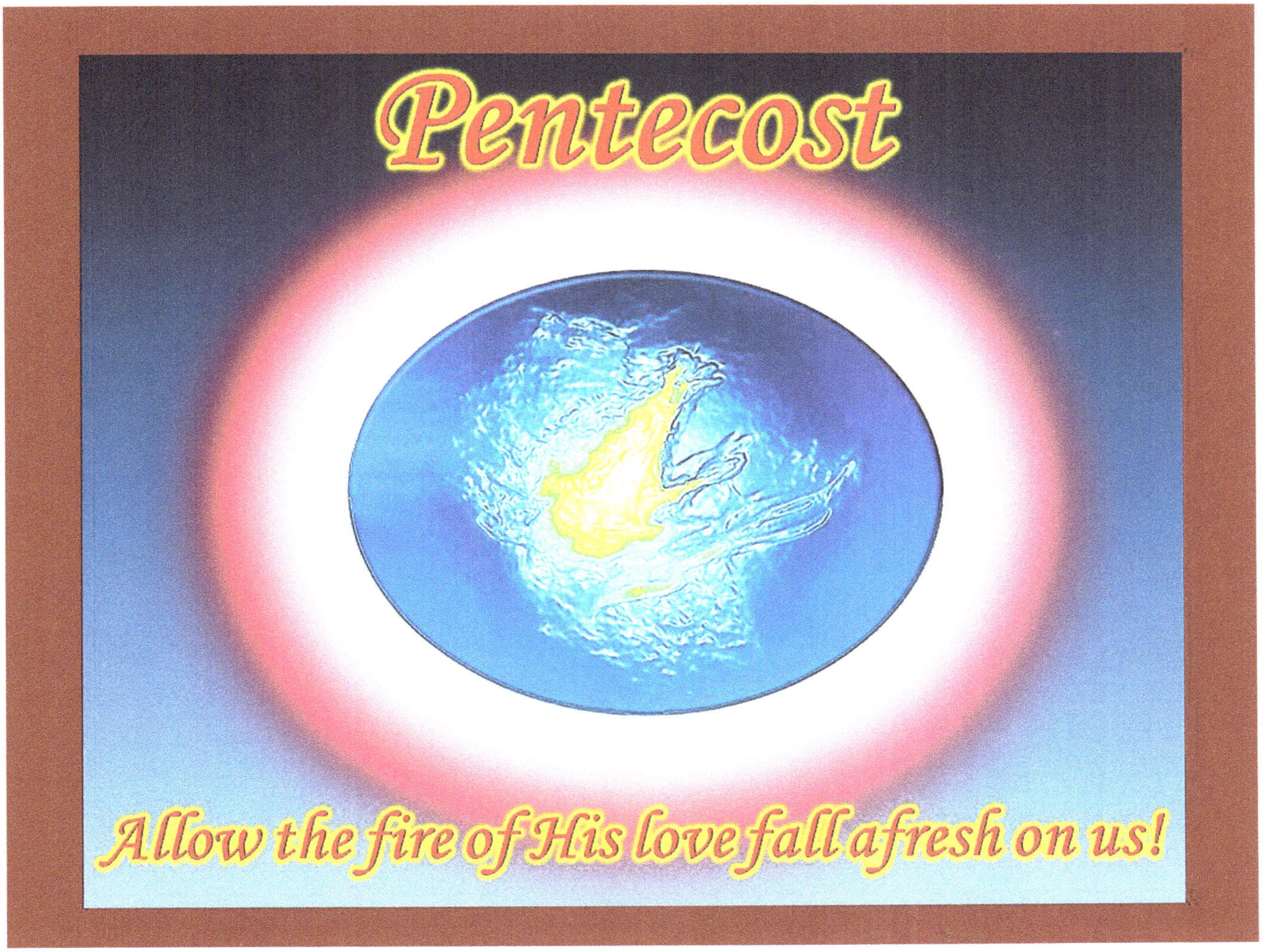
Pentecost
Allow the fire of His love fall afresh on us!

He said to them,
"Come after me, and I will make you
fishers of men."
At once they left their
nets and followed him.

Matthew 4: 19

O Lord, our Lord,
how awesome is your name
through all the earth!

You have set your majesty
above the heavens!
Psalm 8: 2

Wonderful Magnificent God, Beautiful Redeemer You Are!

*Do not store up for yourselves treasures
on earth, where moth and decay destroy,
and thieves break in and steal.
But store up treasures in heaven,
where neither moth nor decay destroy,
nor thieves break in and steal.
For where your treasure is,
there also will your heart be.
Matthew 6:19-21*

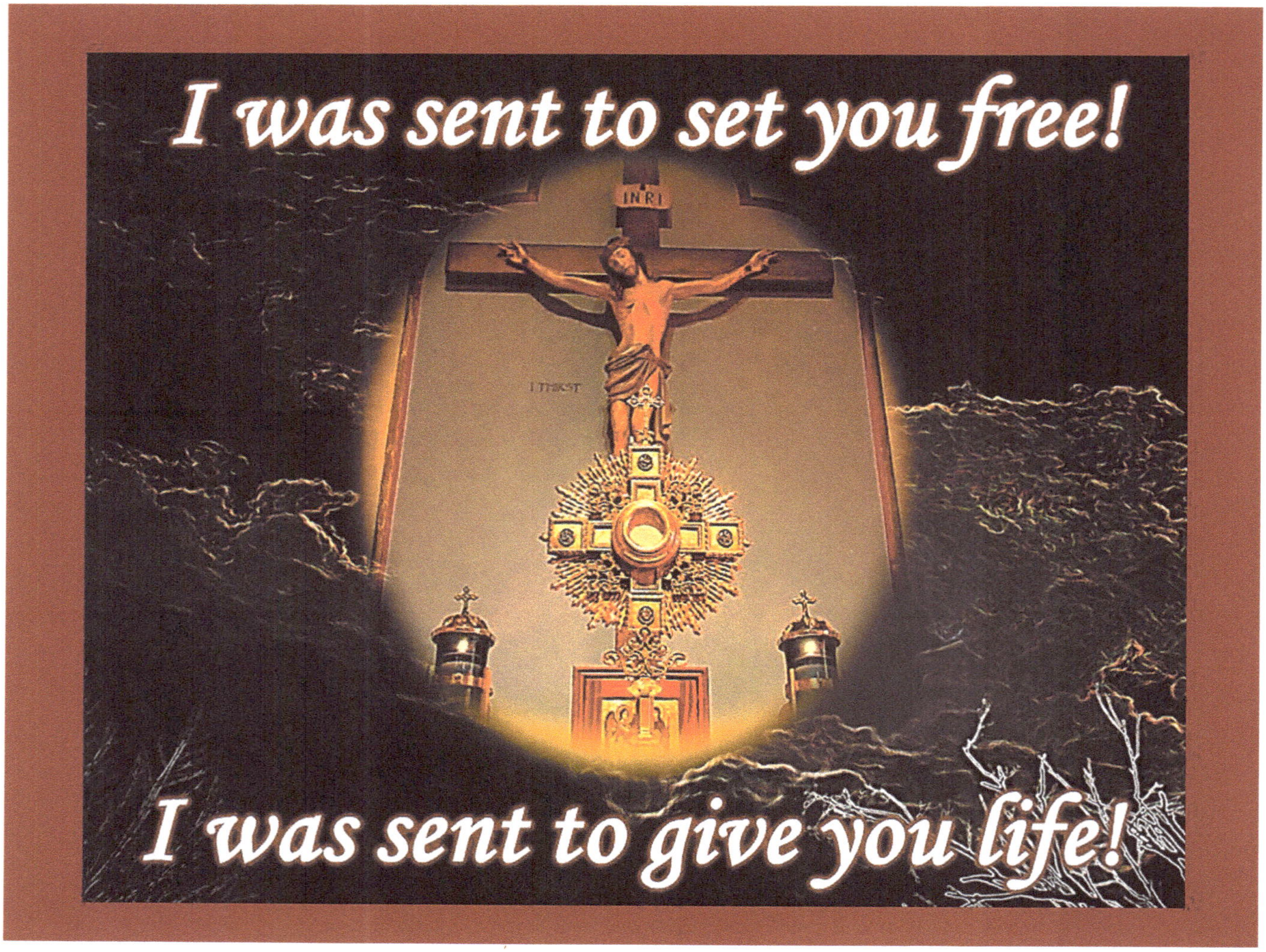
I was sent to set you free!
INRI
I was sent to give you life!

When I found your words,
I devoured them;
they became my joy
and the happiness of my heart.

Jeremiah 15: 16

Remain faithful until death,
and I will give you the crown of life.

Kingdom of Heaven

Revelation 1: 10

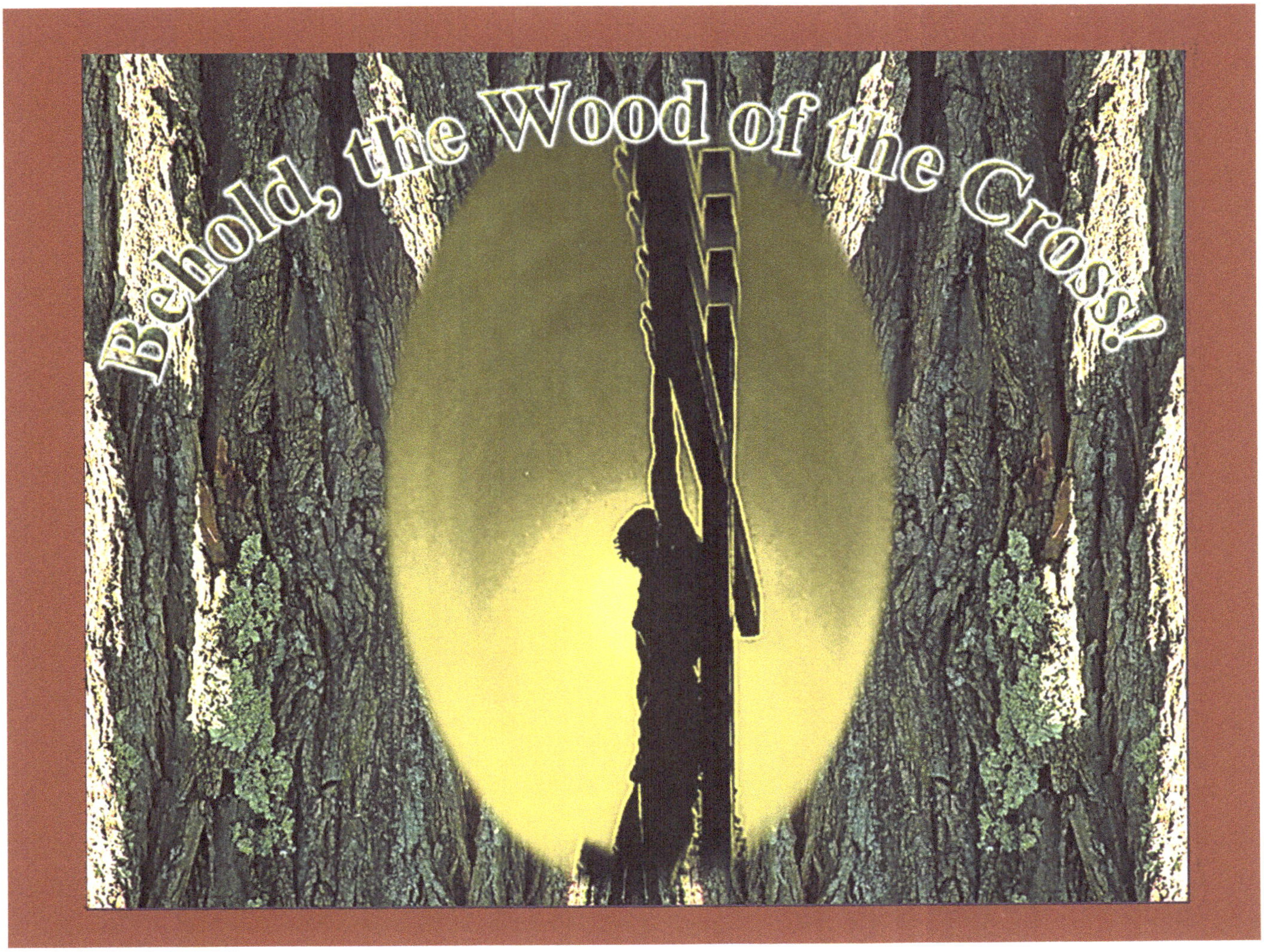
Behold, the Wood of the Cross!

For there is one God.
There is also one mediator
between God
and the human race,
Christ Jesus,
himself human,
who gave himself as ransom for all.

1 Timothy 2: 5-6

The Lord is your guardian;
the Lord is your shade at your
right hand. By day the sun
cannot harm you, nor the moon
by night.
The Lord will guard you from all evil,
will always guard your life. The Lord
will guard your coming and going both
now and forever.
Psalm 121: 5-8

Be sober and vigilant.
Your opponent the devil is prowling
around like a roaring lion
looking for someone to devour.

Resist him, be steadfast in faith.
1 Peter 5: 8-9

Draw near to God, and He will draw near to you!

James 4: 8

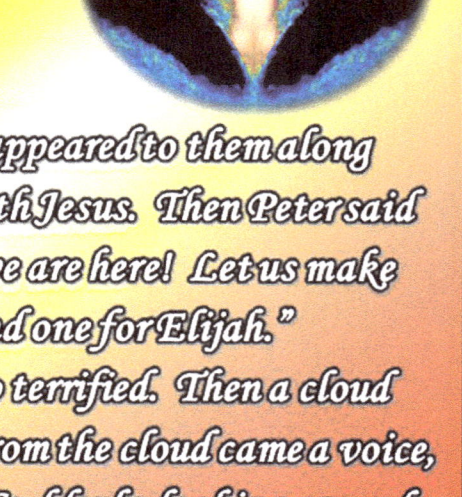

After six days Jesus took Peter, James, and John and led them up a high mountain apart by themselves. And he was transfigured before them, and his clothes became dazzling white, such as no fuller on earth could bleach them. Then Elijah appeared to them along with Moses, and they were conversing with Jesus. Then Peter said to Jesus in reply, "Rabbi, it is good that we are here! Let us make three tents: one for you, one for Moses, and one for Elijah." He hardly knew what to say, they were so terrified. Then a cloud came, casting a shadow over them; then from the cloud came a voice, "This is my beloved Son. Listen to him." Suddenly, looking around, they no longer saw anyone but Jesus alone with them.

Mark 9:2-8

What is your greatest fear?

Know that I Love You!
Know that I am within you!
Know that I go before you!

You are never alone!

For while your obedience is known to all,
so that I rejoice over you,
I want you to be wise as to what is good,
and simple as to what is evil;
then the God of peace
will quickly crush Satan under your feet.
The grace of our Lord Jesus be with you.

Romans 16:19-20

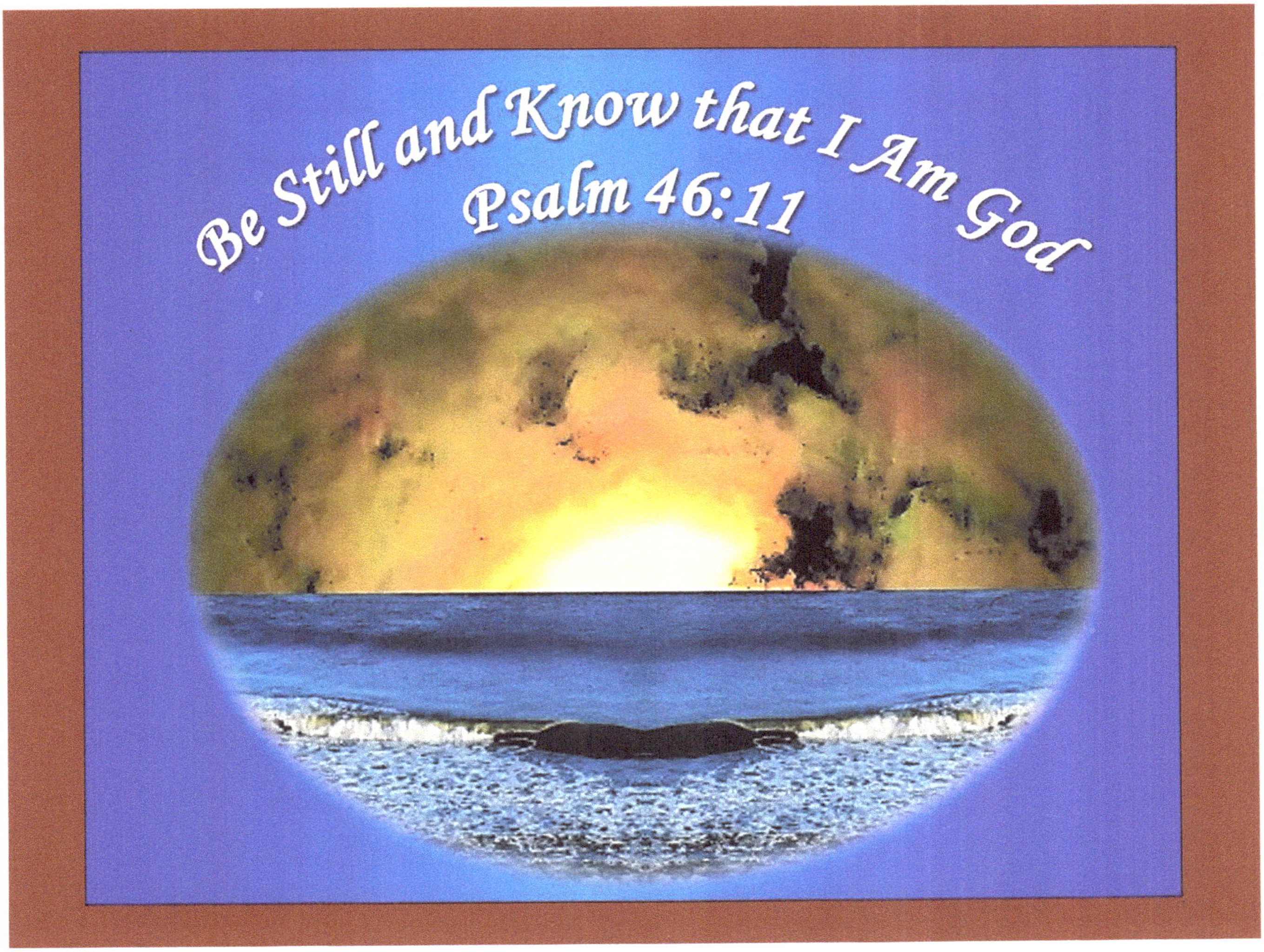
Be Still and Know that I Am God
Psalm 46:11

For by grace you have been saved
through faith, and this is not from you;
it is the gift of God; it is not from works,
so no one may boast.
For we are his handiwork, created in
Christ Jesus for the good works
that God has prepared in advance,
that we should live in them.

Ephesians 2:8-10

Praise, you servants of the Lord,
praise the name of the Lord.
Blessed be the name of the Lord

JESUS

both now and forever.
From the rising of the sun to its setting,
let the name of the Lord be praised.

Whoever believes in me, as scripture says:
"Rivers of living water will flow
from within him"

John 7: 38

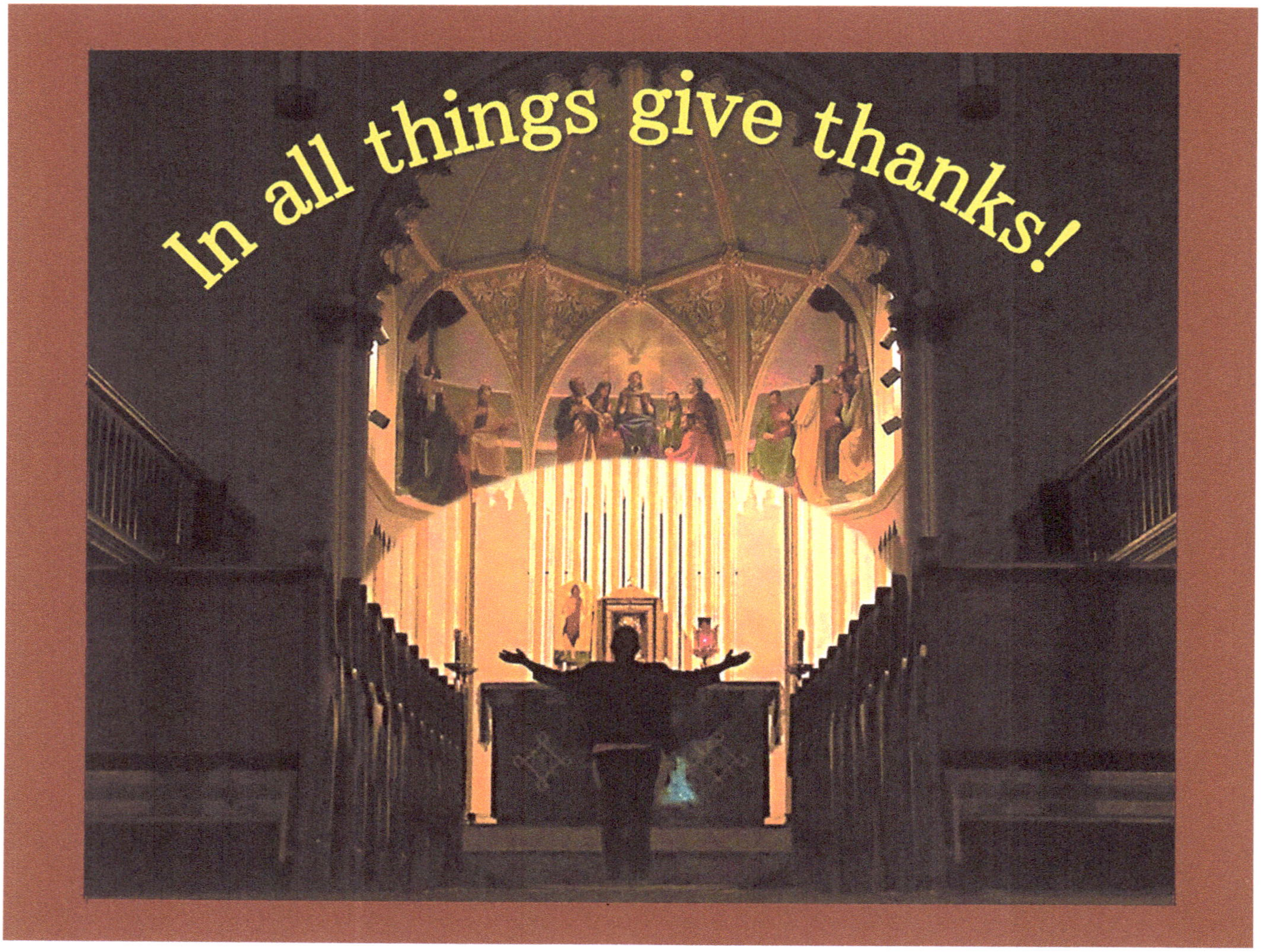
In all things give thanks!

So I look to you in the sanctuary to see your power and glory. For your love is better than life; my lips offer you worship! I will bless you as long as I live; I will lift up my hands, calling on your name. My soul shall savor the rich banquet of praise, with joyous lips my mouth shall honor you!

Psalm 63:3-6

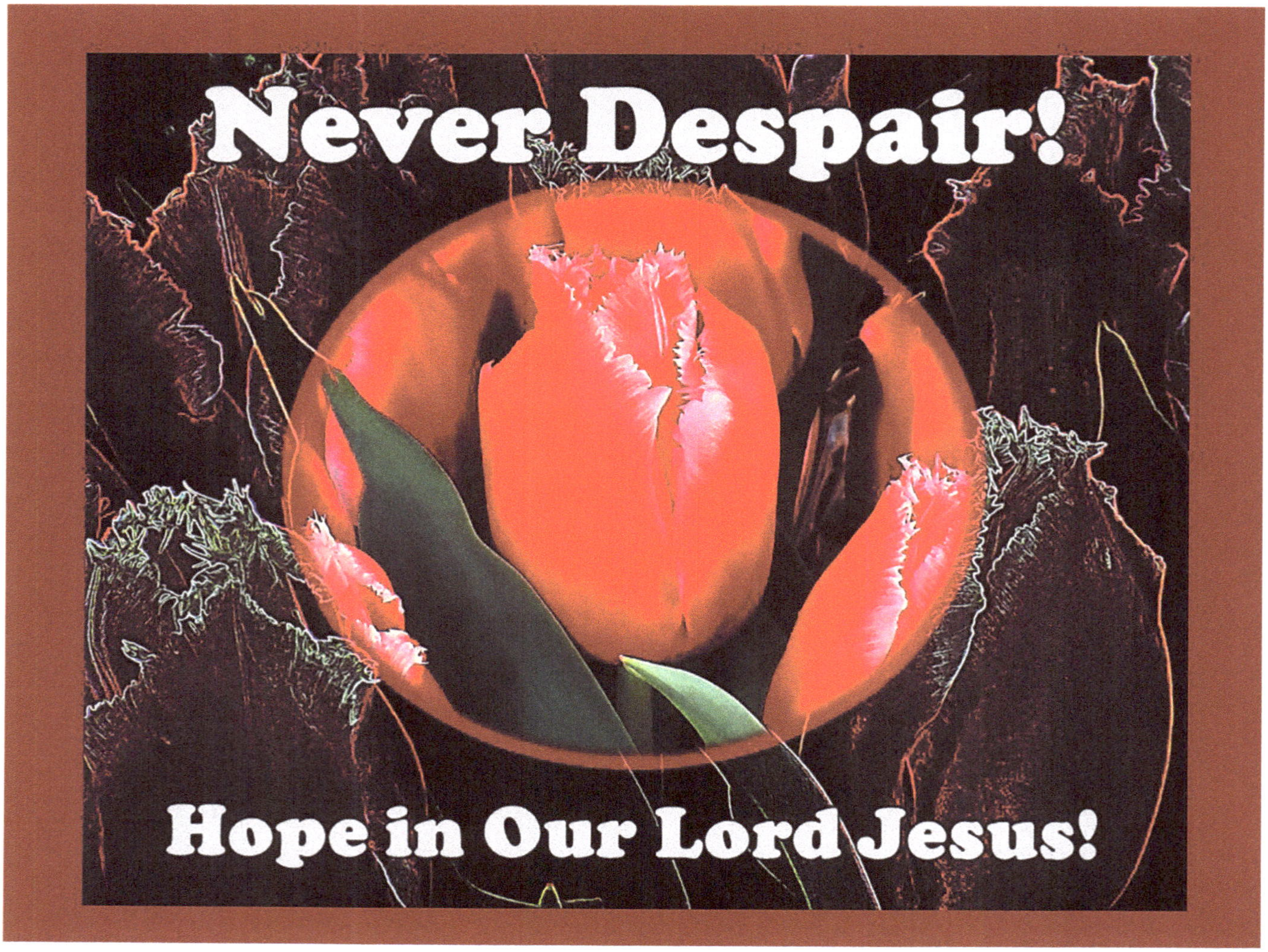
Never Despair!
Hope in Our Lord Jesus!

Consider it all joy, my brothers,
when you encounter various trials,
for you know that the testing of your
faith produces perseverance.
And let perseverance be perfect,
so that you may be perfect and
complete, lacking in nothing.

James 1:2-4

Reflections:

Jesus

Faith – Hope - Love!

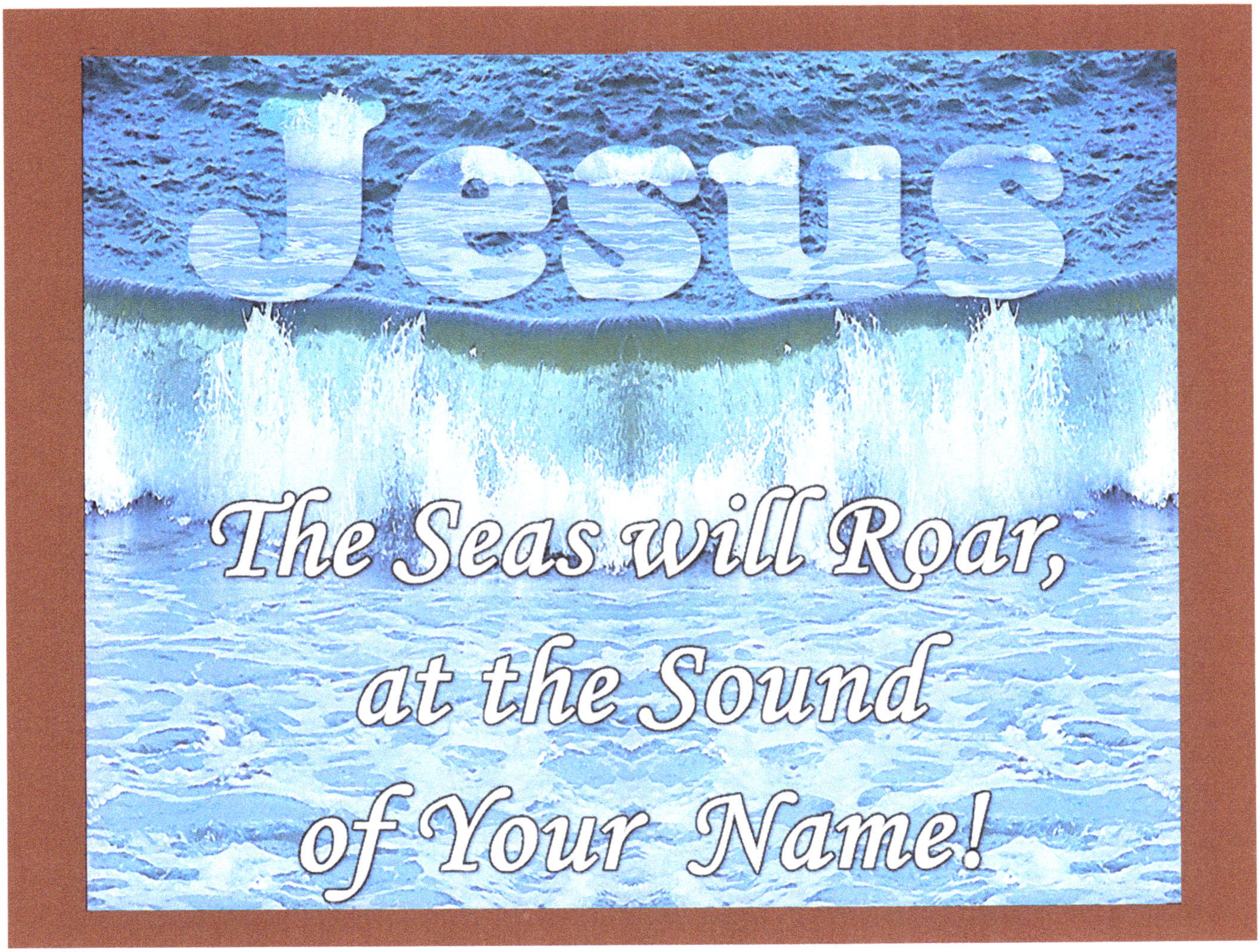

The Seas will Roar,
at the Sound
of Your Name!

Falling down before him,
She explained in the presence of all the people
why she had touched him
and how she had been healed immediately.
He said to her, "Daughter, your faith has saved
you; go in peace."

Luke 8: 47-48

When we touch and consume
the Eucharist (the presence of Jesus)
our faith can heal us as well!
Believe and be healed!

God knows what is done in secret,
in our thought, by our word,
and through our deeds!

For God did not call us to impurity
but to holiness.

Be holy because I Am Holy!

1 Thessalonians 4: 7

The Heart of Love

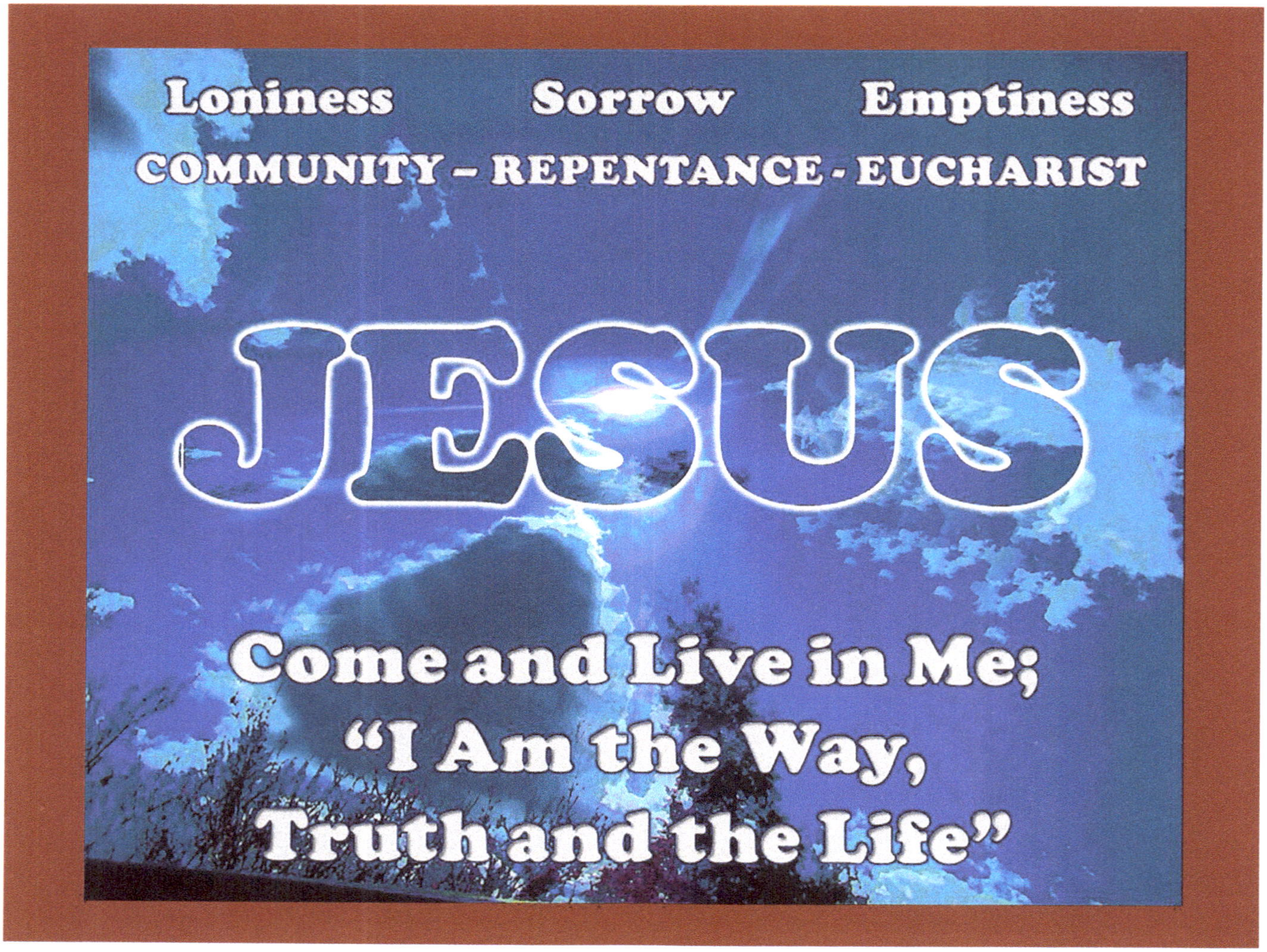

Loniness   Sorrow   Emptiness
COMMUNITY – REPENTANCE - EUCHARIST

JESUS

Come and Live in Me;
"I Am the Way,
Truth and the Life"

For God did not call us
to impurity
but to holiness.

1 Thessalonians 4:7

It is written in the prophets:

Eucharist

'They shall all be taught by God.'
Everyone who listens to my Father and learns from him comes to me.
Not that anyone has seen the Father except the one who is from
God; he has seen the Father. Amen, amen, I say to you,
whoever believes has eternal life. I am the bread of life.
Your ancestors ate the manna in the desert, but they died;
this is the bread that comes down from heaven
so that one may eat it and not die.
I am the living bread that came down from heaven;
whoever eats this bread will live forever; and the bread that I will
give is my flesh for the life of the world."
John 6: 45-51

"The Lord is Compassionate and Merciful."

James 5: 11

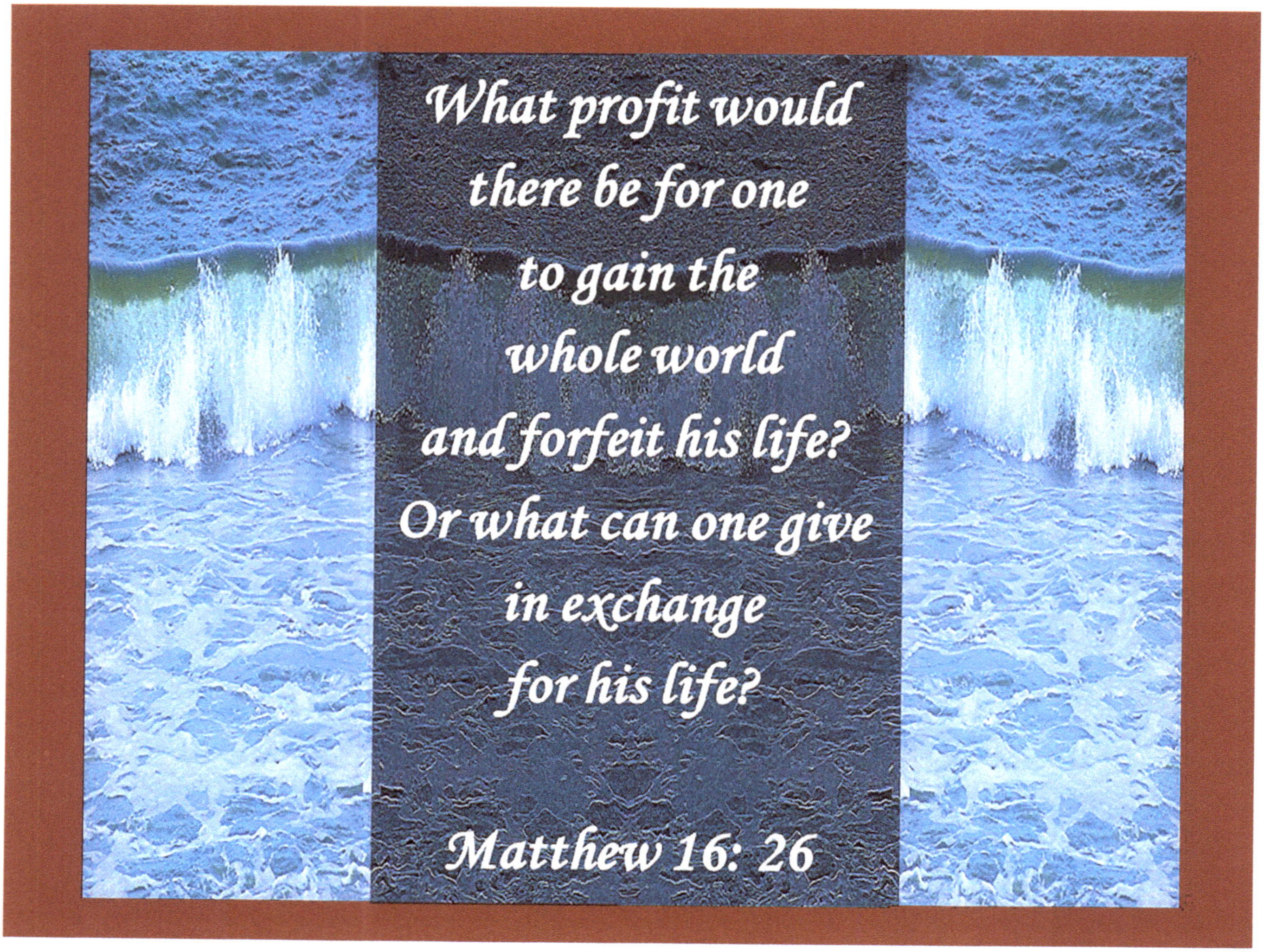

What profit would
there be for one
to gain the
whole world
and forfeit his life?
Or what can one give
in exchange
for his life?

Matthew 16: 26

In the Name of

JESUS

the lame walk, the deaf hear, and the mute speak!

All good giving and every perfect
gift is from above,
coming down from the Father
of lights, with whom here is no
alteration or shadow caused by
change.
He willed to give us birth
by the word of truth
that we may be a kind
of first fruits of his creatures.

James 1: 17-18

Then Moses stretched out his hand over the sea,
and the Lord swept the sea with a strong east wind
throughout the night and so turned it into dry land.

Walk of Faith

When the water was thus divided,
the Israelites marched into the midst of the sea
on dry land, with the water like a wall to their right
and to their left.

Exodus 14: 21-22

He wore a cloak that had been dipped
in blood,
and his name was called the Word of God.
Revelation 19:13

The Sword of the Spirit
is the Word of God!

Ephesians 6:17

*Whoever preaches
let it be with the words of God;
whoever serves,
let it be with the strength that God supplies,
so that in all things
God may be glorified through Jesus Christ,
to whom belong glory and dominion
forever and ever. Amen.*

1 Peter 4:11

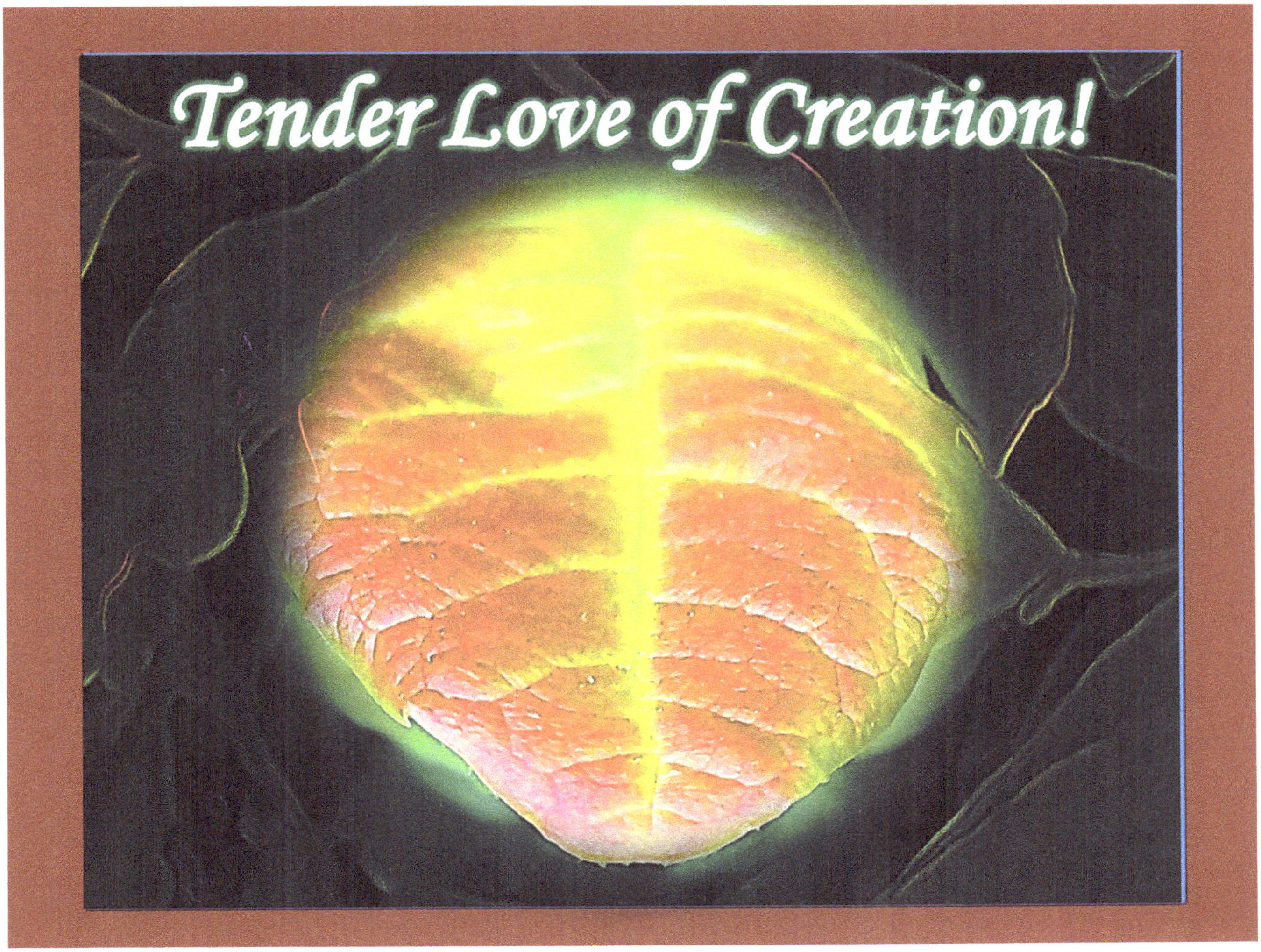
Tender Love of Creation!

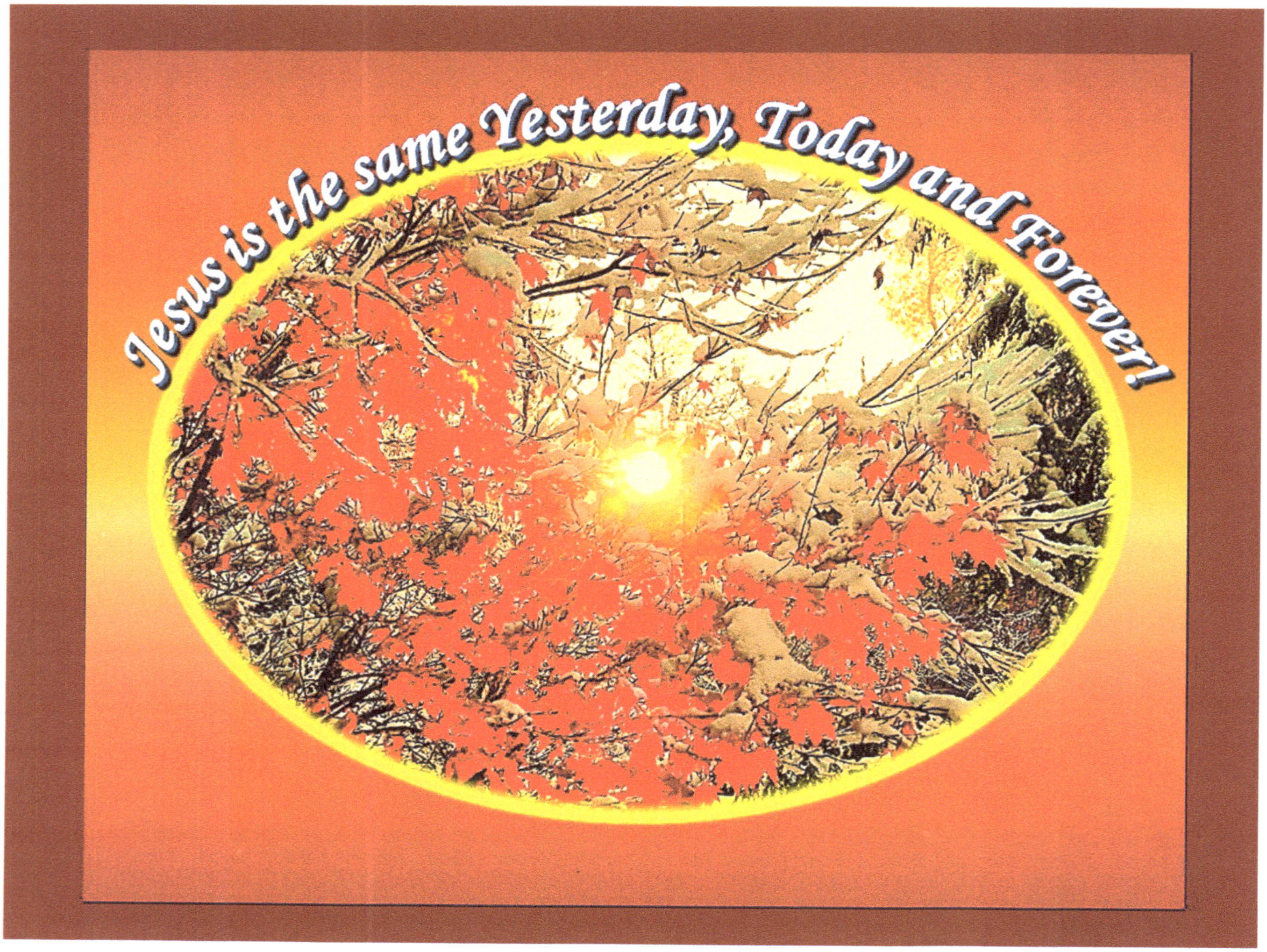
Jesus is the same Yesterday, Today and Forever!

My brothers,
if anyone among you
should stray from
the truth and someone
bring him back,
he should know that
whoever brings back a sinner
from the error of his way will save his soul
from death and will cover
a multitude of sins.
James 5:19-20

Do not conform yourselves to this age but be transformed by the renewal of your mind, that you may discern what is the will of God, what is good and pleasing and perfect.

Romans 12:2

When Raphael entered the house,
Tobit greeted him first. Raphael said,
"Hearty greetings to you!"
Tobit replied: "What joy is left for me anymore?
Here I am, a blind man who cannot see God's sunlight, but
must remain in darkness,
like the dead who no longer see the light!
Though alive, I am among the dead. I can hear a man's
voice, but I cannot see him.
Raphael said, "Take courage!
God has healing in store for you; so take courage!"
Tobit 5:10

Finally, draw your strength from the Lord and from his mighty power. Put on the armor of God so that you may be able to stand firm against the tactics of the devil. For our struggle is not with flesh and blood but with the principalities, with the powers, with the world rulers of this present darkness, with the evil spirits in the heavens. Therefore, put on the armor of God, that you may be able to resist on the evil day and, having done everything, to hold your ground. So stand fast with your loins girded in truth, clothed with righteousness as a breastplate, and your feet shod in readiness for the gospel of peace. In all circumstances, hold faith as a shield, to quench all [the] flaming arrows of the evil one. And take the helmet of salvation and the sword of the Spirit, which is the word of God.

Ephesians 6:10-17

Yesterday, Today, and Forever, His Love for You Never Ends!

Hands of Father Joe Irwin, a Priest forever, my friend and Pastor, may he rest in peace! Amen!

PERSONAL REFLECTIONS

PERSONAL REFLECTIONS

PERSONAL REFLECTIONS

www.ingramcontent.com/pod-product-compliance
Lightning Source LLC
Chambersburg PA
CBHW041115120626

46547CB00019B/2723